J. Roswell Flower

J. Roswell Flower

A Brief Biography

by
DAVID K. RINGER

Foreword by Wayne Warner

WIPF & STOCK · Eugene, Oregon

J. ROSWELL FLOWER
A Brief Biography

Copyright © 2016 David K. Ringer. All rights reserved. Except for brief quotations in critical publications or reviews, no part of this book may be reproduced in any manner without prior written permission from the publisher. Write: Permissions, Wipf and Stock Publishers, 199 W. 8th Ave., Suite 3, Eugene, OR 97401.

Wipf & Stock
An Imprint of Wipf and Stock Publishers
199 W. 8th Ave., Suite 3
Eugene, OR 97401

www.wipfandstock.com

PAPERBACK ISBN 13: 978-1-4982-3128-2
HARDCOVER ISBN 13: 978-1-4982-8803-3

Manufactured in the U.S.A.   02/16/2016

Dedicated to
David W. Flower
and
in memoriam
Adele Flower Dalton

Contents

Foreword by Wayne Warner | ix
Preface | xiii
Acknowledgment | xv
Introduction | xvii

1 Early Life and Faith | 1
2 Marriage and an Epoch Making Meeting | 9
3 First Secretary of the General Council | 18
4 Secretary of the Missionary Department | 27
5 The Eastern District Decade: Pastor and Superintendent | 35
6 Return to National Office | 46
7 Avoiding Sectarianism | 58
8 Historian and Statesman | 68
   Conclusion and Legacy | 79

Appendix A: "Preamble and Resolution on Constitution" | 85
Appendix B: "Back to Calvary" | 88
Appendix C: "One Great Christian Essential: 'Be Filled with the Spirit.'" | 91
Appendix D: "Spreading the Pentecostal Flames" | 94

Chronology | 95
A Note on Sources | 97
Images | 98
For Further Reading | 105

Foreword

DAVID RINGER HAS METICULOUSLY traced the life of an extraordinary man who, after his Christian conversion and surrender to God's plan, became a devoted follower of Jesus and role model for many ministers and lay people in and outside the Assemblies of God. That man was Joseph Roswell Flower.

This brief biography of Flower's long and storied ministerial career shows the story in biography form is long overdue. Its pages will furnish resources for the scholar, inspiration for the lay person, and will challenge this and future generations.

When the Assemblies of God proudly introduced William Menzies' history, *Anointed to Serve*, at the denomination's 1971 General Council, it was the first published history in twenty years. And when readers opened to the dedication page, they saw a photo of J. Roswell Flower and the inscription "Dedicated to the Memory of Joseph Roswell Flower, A Father in the Faith."

For those who knew anything about the man, the selection of Flower seemed very fitting. Thomas F. Zimmerman, general superintendent at the time of Flower's death a year earlier, said Flower's name was "synonymous with the Assemblies of God."

That gives us a glimpse of Flower's importance to the Assemblies of God and the kingdom.

Flower was a founder and active member of the Assemblies of God for fifty-six years. He not only helped organize it, but he also was elected the first general secretary—at the age of twenty-five. He never saw any reason to join another group—except in

Foreword

unity with the National Association of Evangelicals, Pentecostal Fellowship of North America, Pentecostal World Conference, and other interdenominational groups.

He was a man of many talents and gifts: writer, editor, evangelist, church founder, pastor, general officer, and district superintendent. Key experiences that helped him in his national leadership positions.

He was involved in civil responsibilities as well. At the encouragement of friends, he ran for a position on Springfield, Missouri's city council. He won the election and served from 1953 to 1961.

Friends and colleagues in 1970 agreed that he was a father in the faith, but they could also honor him in other ways. If asked to come up with a word or two, one colleague would commend him for his focus while another would quickly mention his family life. Still another would underscore his Christian ethics. And they could list many others.

Let us take a closer look at these selected characteristics of the man for whom this biography is written.

Indeed he was focused. When he became a believer at the age of nineteen, he swung 180 degrees from secular ambitions to a higher calling. And when he surrendered his life to God, he never took it back.

With little formal Bible training, he began to preach and teach and then launched and edited the weekly *Christian Evangel* to extend his ministry to near and far-away places. He saw the power of the printed page, learned to operate the press, and he and his wife Alice filled the paper's columns with articles from other leaders, testimonies, and with their own writings. To some readers, it was their introduction to the Pentecostal experience. To others it brought needed teaching and sorted out some of the misconceptions of the Pentecostal movement.

But he did confess that the movement needed guidance.

When he saw an announcement of a proposed organizational meeting of Pentecostals in Hot Springs, Arkansas, in April 1914, he reprinted it in his paper and attended what became the General

Foreword

Council of the Assemblies of God. And in those early years he contributed no small part in its development and kept it on track and away from hobbies and false doctrines.

He was a man with a Christian focus.

Looking at the memoirs of J. Roswell and Alice's six children, it is easy to see where they received their godly family values. Others could see it too—like Donald Gee, the highly respected English preacher and writer, for example. Gee asked Flower about his secret of the extraordinary family legacy. Ringer writes: "Flower responded that he wasn't sure but decided that two things were important: the daily family altar and his and Alice's efforts to live consistent lives, to live at home as they lived in the pulpit, at church, at Bible camp, and so forth, to live lives of true biblical holiness."

Their missionary daughter Adele in a magazine article added to her father's answer to Gee: "Dad has been an unflickering flame of godliness, of self-effacement, of loyalty, and of undeviating consistency that has inspired me throughout my life."

Their youngest son, David, served as a pastor and district superintendent. He wants his parents remembered as "godly, consistent, honest, and dedicated parents who loved and cared for people." And he added, "They were people who gave of themselves."

How pleased the parents must have been when the children followed them into the ministry.

When Flower left the national office in 1925—he would be back ten years later—he left Springfield with a decision that spoke of his Christian ethics. He had accepted a pastorate in Scranton, Pennsylvania, which would make it extremely difficult to pick up his family of eight, move to a city hundreds of miles away, and minister to a congregation they did not know.

But then the local assembly in Springfield stepped in when they knew Flower was available and offered him their pastorate. He would not have to move and would stay among friends. The offer sounded too good to be true.

But Flower looked at the offer another way. "I have given my word to the church in Scranton," he replied. The Springfield church, which later became Central Assembly, did not really know

Foreword

Flower. They suggested that he go to Scranton for a year and then return to Missouri. Flower ended that conversation by saying, "If I went with such intentions, I would be unworthy to be their pastor."

He ministered in the East for the next ten years.

And in his closing years when he held only the position of honorary presbyter, Flower was still motivated to do what was right and ethical. It came when a leader was dismissed from a position with the denomination. "They were dismissed without a hearing," he told me. "And I'm not through with this case yet."

It isn't known what action he took, but it is certain that his successors knew how strongly he felt about it. Being ethical was not out of style. Nor should it ever be.

Perhaps it was the last biblical lesson from the aged "Father in the Faith" to some of his "children."

Wayne Warner

Preface

I DID NOT GROW up in the Assemblies of God, not even in a Pentecostal denomination. After becoming a Pentecostal, I began attending an Assemblies of God congregation where I met and married a granddaughter of J. Roswell Flower. He had died a decade earlier and I knew very little about him. It was an offhand remark made by my father-in-law about one of his father's achievements that planted the seed of this book in my mind more than thirty years ago. I regret it has taken so long for that seed to bear fruit. The quality of Flower's spiritual and intellectual life, the range of his work as a church and civic leader, and the generosity of his spirit, even to those who disagreed with him, make his life story one worth telling. My desire is that this book will make him and some of his contributions to the kingdom of God better known.

Many people helped make this work a reality, though, none of them is responsible for any weaknesses or errors in it. Wayne Warner, Darrin Rodgers, Joyce Lee, and Glenn Gohr of the Flower Pentecostal Heritage Center assisted in the research and writing at various stages. I offer special thanks to Wayne for his kind and insightful Foreword. Friends Freddy Boswell, John Korstad, Thomas Luiskutty, Nathan Meleen, Hubert Morken, and Gary Pranger prayed for and encouraged me. Three mentors guided an academic version of the story, the late Dr. William W. Menzies and Drs. Stanley M. and Ruth V. Burgess. Their patience and persistence are deeply appreciated; so, too, is the gracious help of

Preface

Dr. Lois Olena, Doctor of Ministry Project Director, Assemblies of God Theological Seminary. The financial and time demands of research and writing were borne with extraordinary patience by my family. Only they know the debt of gratitude I owe them.

Acknowledgment

Grateful acknowledgment is made for the generous permission of the Gospel Publishing House, Springfield, Missouri, for use of substantial excerpts from the following *Pentecostal Evangel* articles by J. Roswell Flower: "Back To Calvary," October 5, 1935; "One Great Christian Essential: 'Be Filled with the Spirit,'" August 5, 1939; and "Spreading the Pentecostal Flames," July 14, 1968.

All Scripture quotations are from the King James Version of the Holy Bible.

Introduction

MORE THAN A CENTURY has passed since the beginning of the modern Pentecostal movement. The origins of Pentecostalism are still contested among scholars, and who should be called the father of the movement is also debated. In the last two decades studies of the movement and some early leaders have proliferated in the Americas, Europe, and other portions of the world where Pentecostals have become a significant force in the Christian church. Several of the first-generation leaders of the movement wrote autobiographies. Others have been the subject of biographies. J. Roswell Flower was a significant founding father and longtime leader in the Pentecostal community; yet, he neither wrote an account of his life nor has he been the focus of a biography other than brief articles, pamphlets, and entries in reference works. Examining his life provides insights into the man, the Assemblies of God, and the larger Pentecostal movement over nearly two-thirds of the twentieth century.

FAMILY ORIGINS

Joseph James Roswell Flower was born June 17, 1888 in Belleville, Ontario, Canada, the first child of George Lorenzo and Bethia Adella (Rice) Flower. He died July 23, 1970 in Springfield, Missouri, USA. His ancestor Lamrock Flower migrated from England to Connecticut around 1660. A descendent of Lamrock married a woman whose forefather, William Brewster, arrived on

Introduction

the *Mayflower*. J. Roswell had this bit of family history officially verified. The first evidence about Flower's religious heritage comes from a newspaper notice of his grandfather's death. Joseph Manly Flower had moved to Canada from New York as a young man to work in the logging industry. In 1853, a few months after the birth of his third child, George (J. Roswell's father), Joseph was mortally wounded trying to loosen a log jam. He lingered for three days in great pain. Without complaining or murmuring, he held steadfastly to his hope of eternal life through the Lord Jesus Christ. Greatly admired for his integrity and exemplary life, a large crowd gathered in the local Congregational Church for his funeral.

Joseph Manly's widow and children were cared for by members of her family for the next few years. When she died before George's tenth birthday, he was sent to live with an aunt who took him to a Presbyterian Church. As a young adult, George longed for a more vibrant relationship with Christ than he found among the Presbyterians. He discovered that vital life at a Methodist Church where he became very active in a prayer band and in evangelism. His fervent life attracted the attention of the minister's daughter, Bethia Adella Rice. Bethia's father, James Joseph Rice Jr. was the son of a Welsh man who had come to Newfoundland, Canada on business and stayed. A loyal member of the Church of England (Anglican), he raised his children in the church. However, James Jr. and his wife became Methodists following the death at age fourteen of their oldest child. This son had been injured as a schoolboy and was an invalid. Members of the local Methodist ("Bible Christians") congregation visited him; he found great comfort and assurance in the faith they taught him. James Joseph and his wife also found joy in that faith. Sometime after their conversion, he began preaching and was sent by church officials to the Holloway Methodist Church in Belleville as the pastor, where George and Bethia became acquainted.

At the time of their meeting, she was engaged to a man she increasingly realized she did not love. One of her older brothers saw her unhappiness and perplexity and helped her break the engagement. Drawn to each other spiritually as well as in other

Introduction

ways, George and Bethia did not seem to mind the twelve-year age difference between them. He was thirty-four and she twenty-two when they married in 1887. The couple moved into the house in which George had been born and in which J. Roswell arrived a year later.

BACKGROUND

Flower was significantly influenced by the situation in Canada during his childhood and early youth. Canada was sharply divided between an English-speaking, Protestant population and a Roman Catholic, French-speaking one, primarily in Quebec. Ontario, home of the Flowers, was predominantly Protestant and English-speaking. Public life, especially education, reflected the tensions between the two sectarian groups. However, the large migrations of other European peoples to Canada in the latter decades of the 1800s necessitated a significant shift in public education from faith-based character-development to national unity and Canadianizing the new immigrants. This refocusing of the goal of education somewhat secularized the ethos of the schools and emphasized the common good over that of individuals and distinct groups—religious, linguistic, or ethnic. At about the same time J. Roswell began his formal education in the 1890s, Canadians elected a Roman Catholic Prime Minister. Flower was influenced by these elements of Canada's public life. He remained a foe of sectarianism all his life; he had a larger sense of the common good in public life than most American fundamentalists; and he ever treasured democracy in politics and religion.

The event that would come to have the defining impact on his life and ministry occurred in Topeka, Kansas, when J. Roswell was but twelve years old. On January 1, 1901 Agnes N. Ozman (LaBerge) spoke in tongues. She, her classmates at Bethel Bible School, and their teacher, Charles F. Parham, believed that tongues-speech was the initial, physical evidence of the baptism in the Holy Spirit. They were seeking God for the experience in an evening service when Ozman was Spirit-baptized. Years later, Flower wrote that it

Introduction

was that event and that interpretation of it that began the twentieth-century Pentecostal movement. The fire of that revival spread from Kansas to Houston, Texas and on to Los Angeles, California where it burned intensely between 1906 and 1909, becoming a worldwide conflagration. In 1907 the fire was carried from Azusa Street to Indianapolis, Indiana where J. Roswell Flower and Alice Marie Reynolds would enter the Pentecostal movement.

The third major influence on Flower's early years was his father's conduct of family life. George Flower daily read the Bible to and prayed with his family. He read the Scriptures chapter by chapter, exposing his son and daughter to much if not all of the Bible. He also took his family to church regularly, but not always to the same church. George and Bethia Flower were ever in search of a more vibrant Christian fellowship where holy living was demonstrated. They left Methodism for the Plymouth Brethren. In the latter Sunday school J. Roswell memorized Isaiah 53. His father also sent him to a Presbyterian church where he learned the catechism (probably *The Westminster Shorter Catechism*). Later, when the family moved to Toronto, they attended a congregation of John Alexander Dowie's followers. Impressed with these congregants, George moved his family to Zion City, Illinois, home of the Dowie community. J. Roswell recalled the double impact of his father's leadership: the regularity of daily Bible reading and prayer stabilized life; the constant changing of churches created a "scattered, wandering spirit."

PURPOSE

In 1940 J. Roswell Flower published an article in the *CA Herald* titled "There Was a Man." He argued that when God wanted to accomplish some specific and essential purpose in his kingdom, he chose a man or a woman (Flower made that explicit in the article) to do the task. I believe Flower was right. It is my conviction that God called J. Roswell and others to participate in his purposes in calling into being the twentieth-century Pentecostal movement

Introduction

(including the Assemblies of God) to spread and to sustain Spirit-empowered expressions of the Christian faith in the world.

1

Early Life and Faith

> We drifted, sometimes going to the Christian and Missionary Alliance, sometimes here and sometimes there; but we more or less drifted until this Pentecostal meeting opened in Indianapolis. That was in January, 1907.
>
> —J. Roswell Flower, "Our Pentecostal Heritage"

LIFE IN ZION CITY

J. ROSWELL BEGAN SCHOOL in the city of his birth, Belleville, Ontario, Canada. When he learned to read, he became an avid, excellent, and life-long reader. As a child he took books from the shelves of his father's general store, read them, and replaced them for sale. The family moved from Belleville to Toronto where J. Roswell completed his required education. Following that, he sat for and passed in 1902 the examination that permitted him to enter a collegiate institute or high school. However, in pursuit of what they hoped were richer spiritual pastures, George and Bethia

J. Roswell Flower

Flower moved their family to Zion City, Illinois, that summer. They hoped to find in the home city of John Alexander Dowie's church the kind of holy living, faith in the healing power of God, and beloved community for which they longed. They were deeply disappointed and moved to Indianapolis, Indiana just two years later.

Zion City did give Flower some opportunities. He did not attend high school there. He did join the prize-winning band led by F. F. Bosworth, playing cornet, and took a stenography course with an eye toward finding employment. His training and ability to take shorthand, to write well, and to edit became important aspects of his work in God's kingdom. The location of Zion City provided opportunity for adventure for the teenage boy. He and a friend, W. O. Boyd, decided to take an excursion down the nearby Plaines River in a rowboat. They traveled several miles before deciding their scheme was ill-conceived and returned home. What the city did not offer the Flowers, and J. Roswell in particular, was a spiritual home. In fact, he became spiritually lethargic. He did submit to water baptism. Later, he referred to the event as a "ducking," not a genuine baptism.

Disillusioned by the quality of the spiritual life among his followers and Dowie's claim to be the First Apostle of the Christian Catholic Church, the family moved to Ben Davis, Indiana, a small community outside of Indianapolis, now part of the city. The move to Indiana was not to find new spiritual pasture, but for George to take employment connected to the business of a relative. Once more the family was adrift spiritually. J. Roswell lost interest in religious matters. He did not rebel against his parents. However, he became "worldly," attending movies, smoking, and irregularly attending church, whichever one his parents happened to be attending at the time. He found it difficult to work, sometimes being fired for the poor quality of his work and more often simply quitting. About 1906 he found employment with a lawyer and decided to pursue the reading of law. That was less satisfying than he expected, though he did continue it, and once more he found himself restless, even as his parents continued to be spiritually restless.

Early Life and Faith

LIFE IN INDIANAPOLIS

George and Bethia prospered in their new location. They discovered a small band of hungering disciples among who were two women who had experienced extraordinary healings. Mary Alice Reynolds had been healed on her deathbed in response to the prayer of a Quaker minister. Her Methodist minister silenced her testimony in the church and she sought a fellowship in which her witness would be welcomed. Following her healing she had conceived and given birth to her third child, a daughter, Alice Marie, just two years younger that J. Roswell Flower. Along with others, Mary Alice was leading a prayer group of those seeking a deeper life in Christ. The other woman who received an amazing healing was Anna (Mrs. George) Eldridge; she was healed of advanced tuberculosis. Her husband was a Methodist minister who discovered his wife's testimony was unwelcomed in the church. After a meeting with A. B. Simpson, Eldridge became the minister of the newly formed Christian and Missionary Alliance (CMA) group in Indianapolis. All hungering souls—the Flowers, the Reynolds, and the Eldridges—were drawn into the same fellowship.

One man who had earlier been a part of that loose-knit group was Glenn A. Cook. Cook's spiritual hunger had taken him to the Azusa Street Mission in Los Angeles, California, where he received the Pentecostal baptism in the Holy Spirit. Convicted that he had wronged some people in Indianapolis, Cook returned to make amends. He arrived at the prayer group meeting in the CMA building in January 1907 while the Eldridges were absent and testified to his experience. When the Eldridges warned people to stop attending Cook's meetings and forbade him to use the CMA facilities, those who followed him began meeting in another place. Among those who went to those meetings was Mary Alice Reynolds and her daughter Alice Marie and George and Bethia Flower and their daughter Louisa Bernice, but not their son J. Roswell. Slowly, members of the mission, as they called it, began receiving the baptism in the Holy Spirit. On Easter Sunday, sixteen-year-old Alice Marie Reynolds was prostrated under the power of God

3

J. Roswell Flower

as she was Spirit-baptized and spoke in tongues for more than an hour. J. Roswell's parents were with her.

At home, the Flowers talked about the meetings at the mission and gave an account of Alice Marie's experience. Their son listened but showed no interest in attending. A few weeks after Alice's Spirit-baptism, Bethia Flower also was baptized in the Spirit. The change in her life attracted her son and challenged him, though his parents had not confronted him about his lifestyle. Soon thereafter, J. Roswell stopped in to a Sunday afternoon meeting as he returned from photographing an accident site for the interurban railroad. He was captivated by what he heard and saw. However, in the end, it was his mother's changed life that convicted him and brought him to repentance and faith in Christ. Later, he became aware that his water baptism was not genuine. He, Alice Marie Reynolds, and her mother, Mary Alice Reynolds, were all water baptized in the same service by William Hamner Piper at the Stone Church in Chicago, Illinois.

The new convert began attending the general meetings of the mission and also became a regular at the young people's gatherings. J. Roswell was not working full-time, so he went with the young people on witnessing trips and showed up at social gatherings, especially where there was food and, increasingly, where he knew Alice Marie would be present. The young people participated in two significant forms of witnessing with minimal adult supervision. A number of them, led usually by Alice Reynolds, went to a factory once a week at lunchtime and had a brief service and teaching for the employees. They, also, went out on the streets in the afternoon or evening to conduct services. Some of these meetings were conducted near the Soldiers and Sailors Monument in the center of Indianapolis. Other meetings were held on the streets of outlying towns near the city. They traveled to these places on the public streetcars, sitting in a cluster when possible and singing hymns and choruses as they went. They did the same thing going to picnics in the parks along the river on the west side of the city. Usually, the adults accompanied them on picnics, chaperoning and providing the food. It was on one of these outings that J. Roswell and Alice Marie shared an extraordinary experience of nature, a mystical sense of being lost in the beauty and goodness of nature. Both of them believed that such contact with nature refined and ennobled them and drew them closer to God.

The worship experiences of the new Pentecostal community growing in Indianapolis were formative for Flower and for Alice Reynolds. From the beginning, adults and youth worshipped together. While the adults generally were in charge, both young and old participated in Spirit-inspired and Spirit-empowered activities. Adults and young people stood together and sang in the Spirit (the "heavenly choir"); both laid hands on and prayed for the sick; both prayed for others at the altars; and both gave messages in tongues and interpreted the messages. Alice Reynolds's gift of interpretation of tongues was well-known and accepted. Youth were sometimes given opportunity to teach, especially in the home meetings. J. Roswell led some of these Bible study sessions even before he was Spirit-baptized. The community was also moderately integrated racially. Whites went to meetings in black homes. Flower delighted in the fellowship and worship he experienced among the black saints. Prior to his declaring himself Oneness (Jesus Only), the African-American pastor G. T. Haywood was an important leader among Pentecostals in the city.

GROWING IN CHRIST

J. Roswell Flower had come to faith in Christ without much emotion; nonetheless, he knew something had occurred in his spirit. Furthermore, he believed there were two subsequent "works of grace" he was to experience. He was saved; now he had to move on to sanctification and baptism in the Holy Spirit. This three-stage holiness model of Christian experience was the accepted standard at Azusa Street; it was the model Glenn Cook had brought from there and the one generally accepted in Indianapolis prior to the influence of William H. Durham's "finished work" teaching. Not long after his salvation experience, Flower went to the altar at the close of a meeting to seek sanctification. He claimed it by faith and once again had the assurance something had happened in his soul. He then stood up to testify that he was sanctified. As he began speaking, the joy of his full consecration (the word he later came to prefer) came upon him; he shouted, ran two miles home, and went straight to bed for fear the joy would leave him. It did not.

J. Roswell did not assume that being fully consecrated to God necessarily meant he should go into full-time ministry. However, he did become more active in witnessing and helping others in services: he was an altar worker, praying with those who responded to an altar call, a song leader, and sometimes a Bible teacher. At some point, he became convinced he had a call to missionary service in Africa. What was of far greater significance to him, however, was the need for, and his desire for, the baptism in the Holy Spirit evidenced by speaking in other tongues. For many months he prayed both in tarrying services and at home without achieving his goal. Though he sometimes became discouraged, he did not cease active ministry and learning. With two other young men, Fred Vogler and B. F. Lawrence, he launched out into evangelistic and teaching ministry across the midwestern part of Indiana. During these campaigns a stirring in his heart, an aptitude for pastoral ministry grew. His ability to write and edit stimulated a desire to use the printed page for ministry; at age twenty he began publishing a small magazine titled *Pentecost* in 1908. In the winter of 1909, John G. Lake invited him to come to South Africa to work with him there. This seemed to be circumstantial evidence affirming a missionary call to that field. However, his mother had a dream about this and warned him not to go. He heeded her warning.

Instead of heading for Africa, Flower turned westward with a stop in St. Louis, Missouri in early March of 1909 with plans to journey on to Kansas City where he would work in evangelistic and summer camp efforts with A. S. Copley. The purpose for his stop in St. Louis was to ask Mary "Mother" Moise to write a piece for *Pentecost* on her rescue work among women in the city. His planned brief stay turned into nearly a month-long visit. As he waited on the Lord during those days, he spent much time in the "tarrying room." One day as he prayed, he imagined himself on a parallel track to the Lord. If he continued on his course, he would never receive the baptism in the Holy Spirit. He would have to stop and turn to face the Lord. At that point in his prayer, he physically stood up, turned "toward the Lord," and said, "There Lord, I face you and take from you definitely the gift of the Holy Ghost." As he had claimed his salvation and consecration by faith, he now received Spirit-baptism by faith. This was followed by a keen sense that a work had been done in his soul and that the long sought-for baptism was his. There was only one problem—he did not speak in tongues.

Over the next sixteen months, J. Roswell waited for, anticipated, despaired of, and sought for the initial, physical evidence of baptism in the Holy Spirit. Twice he consciously pronounced a few syllables in what he thought was tongues; once he spoke in tongues in a dream; and once he prayed in tongues for another person. He was unaware of the latter instance—others told him later that it had occurred. In the absence of a conscious instance of tongues-speech, he tried to hold on by faith to the conviction that his experience in St. Louis was the baptism in the Holy Spirit. At one point, when he was asked about it, he denied having received Spirit-baptism. Finally, in July of 1910, praying for another person at a summer Bible camp, he became aware that he was praying in tongues as naturally as he prayed in English. He was filled with joy, a joy that intensified as the day went on.

During those months of waiting for the "evidence" of his Spirit-baptism, he was steadily active in ministry. His work with A. S. Copley ended in the fall of 1909. When he left Kansas City, Flower turned over to Copley the *Pentecost*. For the next several months he poured himself into evangelism at various places in Indiana, Ohio, West Virginia, and Kentucky. Young as he was, others recognized the anointing of God on his life and were open to his ministry of preaching, teaching, intercession, and spiritual counseling. By default, as it were, he was becoming a full-time minister. And just as important if not more so was a growing awareness shared with his parents that they were all finally "home" spiritually. What their hearts had longed for, for so long—solid biblical teaching, vibrant faith and holy living, miraculous workings of God, a loving community of saints, and a deep and intense hope in the imminent coming of the Lord Jesus Christ—was theirs in abundance.

CONCLUSION

As a child in Canada, J. Roswell had received a solid public education and a broad religious one in various churches and Sunday schools as well as at home. In his early- and mid-teen years, he lost interest in spiritual things and, though he had the educational skills needed to be gainfully employed, he found he had no solid interest in any secular field, even the law. Following his conversion near his twentieth birthday, his interest in spiritual matters sprang to life along with a desire to study the Bible. He felt a "fluttering in [his] brain" during a prayer service that he took to be God restoring his mind. From that point on, he grew rapidly in his knowledge of and understanding of the Bible, of spiritual experience, and of historical and theological writings. Ministry filled his thoughts and time. He discovered that as he poured himself into the service of the Lord, his material needs were supplied. However, these wonderful spiritual blessings did not take away J. Roswell's longing for a loving, marital relationship with Alice Marie Reynolds with whom he had fallen in love.

2

Marriage and an Epoch Making Meeting

This meeting in Hot Springs is to take up some important subjects, and promises to be an epoch maker should the assembled ministers handle each question presented in the spirit of love and fellowship.
—J. ROSWELL FLOWER, *CHRISTIAN EVANGEL*, MARCH 28, 1914

LOVE FOR ALICE

KNEELING BY ALICE MARIE Reynolds as she lay on the floor speaking in tongues under the power of the Holy Spirit, George and Bethia Flower hoped their son J. Roswell might find a girl like Alice. A few months later, following his conversion, J. Roswell began to spend time with the young people both in their services and ministry times and in their social gatherings and outings. A year later he confided to his diary that Alice was the "dearest thing on earth" to him. Other girls in the group were close friends and confidants, but only Alice began to have a special place in his heart. He ministered with her at the factory outreach; he observed her exercise of spiritual gifts, especially tongues and interpretation; and he shared nature and poetry with her on outings. At the end of another year, he wrote in his diary that he was hopelessly in love with her and did not know what to do.

By this time Alice had graduated from high school and was taking classes at Butler College (University). She believed that God had called her as a missionary to Africa as a single woman. It was confusing to her when one of the other young men in the group told her that God had told him she was to marry him so they could go to Africa together. On one of the group's picnics, he proposed to her, though she did not give him an answer. J. Roswell heard the news and felt that he had been hit in the chest with a brick. Somewhat later as he prepared to go to St. Louis and Kansas City for a summer of evangelistic and camp work, he wrestled with God's will about his feelings for Alice. Determined to put the whole matter aside in order to focus on the joint ministry he and A. S. Copley planned, he nonetheless had to confess that he loved her and could not imagine how the matter would end.

The months he spent in Missouri were difficult for him as he struggled with the question of his Spirit-baptism. The agony of the struggle was so intense that he wanted to throw himself into the Missouri River to end his misery. He had little communication directly with Alice during that time, but he did hear from others that she rejected her suitor, who subsequently went to Africa without her. The news was some relief to J. Roswell. Nonetheless, God seemed to bring him to the question whether or not he would be willing to live life without Alice. He finally said yes. First, foremost, and always, he determined he wanted to know and do the will of God; nothing else really mattered. Shortly thereafter, he wrote an article for *Pentecost* expressing the spiritual principle God had worked in him. The title of the piece was "Subdued." Six weeks later, he returned to Indianapolis, and to Alice.

When he saw her again, his love "burst into greater flame than ever." Remarkably, Flower remained focused on determining the

Marriage and an Epoch Making Meeting

Lord's will for continuing ministry. He decided to conduct a series of meetings in Greensburg, Indiana, about forty miles southeast of Indianapolis. Prior to going to the town, he went by Alice's home in Indianapolis. Without a specific, conscious intent of doing so, when an opportune moment presented itself, he declared his love for her. She asked him to say nothing further and to keep their relationship at the level of friendship. That, he told her, was not possible. He committed the matter to God and with peace of mind and heart left for Greensburg. Three weeks into his campaign, a number of the young people from the Pentecostal mission in Indianapolis, including Alice, traveled by train to Greensburg to help J. Roswell for a few days. Again, seizing the moment, he proposed to Alice as the two of them were having breakfast together in a hotel dining room. She said yes. The day was Tuesday, February 22, 1910, Washington's Birthday.

The path to the altar was not smooth or fast. Flower wanted to marry that summer. However, Charles Reynolds, Alice's father, thought the couple was too young and untried. She was nineteen and J. Roswell twenty-one. They did not rebel against her father's wishes. Instead, Flower continued to engage in evangelistic campaigns in Ohio, West Virginia, and Kentucky before returning to Indiana. During those months, Alice went through doubts that plunged her betrothed into dark periods. They worked hard to make sure their hearts were yielded to the Lord's will for their lives. What mattered most to them was to live lives that would honor God and be fruitful in his kingdom. With great joy and peace, they married on June 1, 1911. One observer noted of J. Roswell that his face had the look "of an impassioned pilgrim reaching a shrine he journeyed toward many long, weary days." George and Bethia Flower's prayers were answered.

Earlier that day, Thursday, Flower went to the county clerk's office to obtain the marriage license. One question on the application required the groom to state his means of support. He wrote "Philippians 4:19." The clerk asked the meaning of his answer and Flower quoted the verse. The man was intrigued by the response and leaked the incident to the *Indianapolis News* where it was

J. Roswell Flower

published that evening with the heading "His Faith is Strong." For those who did not know the biblical reference, the newspaper printed the verse! ("But my God shall supply all your need according to his riches in glory by Christ Jesus.") For most of the next six decades J. Roswell and Alice Reynolds Flower lived that verse, demonstrating the faithfulness of God to his promise.

LIFE TOGETHER

J. Roswell and Alice began on their wedding night a family altar, a time to read the Bible and pray together. They continued that spiritual exercise all of their lives. When the children came, they were included; if there were guests in the home, they were included; if visitors showed up at the time for the family altar, they were included. Life together meant a life of worship and service.

Before their wedding, they had arranged to borrow a large tent. Soon after they were married, the Flowers took the tent into north central Indiana and spent the summer conducting tent revival services. A small portion of the tent was curtained off to serve as their living quarters. The farmers and others who attended their services brought them produce instead of cash. What they did not need for food, Alice canned. At the end of the summer, they had a barrel full of jars of fruits and vegetables for the winter.

Already, J. Roswell had been nourished by the ministry of older men and women who saw the blessing of God in his life and gladly mentored him. One of those men was David Wesley Myland. He had taught in the Christian and Missionary Alliance mission in Indianapolis as well as the Pentecostal fellowship there. Flower had listened to him and even participated with him in services. Myland's concept of the Pentecostal outpouring as the "latter rain," which he had published in book form in 1910, was widely believed in Pentecostal circles. Flower accepted it as an important type of dispensationalism that specifically supported the continuation of spiritual gifts in modern Christianity. Characterizing the coming of the Holy Spirit on the Day of Pentecost as the "early (former) rain" and the twentieth-century outpouring as the "latter rain," the

Marriage and an Epoch Making Meeting

doctrine remained a key component of Flower's understanding of the twentieth-century Pentecostal movement.

In the fall of 1911 after the tent meetings were concluded, J. Roswell and Alice temporarily moved to Columbus, Ohio to help the Mylands conduct Bible camps and evangelistic meetings. When they returned to Indiana, J. Roswell became the minister of a small Pentecostal congregation in Indianapolis. Several missionaries had already gone out from that assembly. Earlier, he had functioned as the missionary secretary, mailing to the missionaries all the funds given for their support. He began to realize that much more could be done for missions if the various congregations of Pentecostal believers who were in fellowship with each other would voluntarily cooperate by pooling their resources. The nearly rabid fear of Pentecostals of any kind of organization made such cooperation difficult.

Flower had also become aware, much earlier, of the great need for careful teaching among those in the new movement, especially for the younger men and women who were receiving the baptism in the Holy Spirit. Myland, too, saw the need and proposed opening a Bible school in Indiana very near where J. Roswell and Alice were living. Gibeah Bible School opened its doors to a few students for nearly two years in Plainfield, Indiana. Besides the Flowers two other couples who came to be leaders in the Assemblies of God studied at Gibeah and, like the Flowers, were ordained by Myland: the Fred Voglers and Flem Van Meters. J. Roswell and Alice attended classes and services as much as possible. Their schedule became much busier when their first child was born, and they decided to publish a weekly Pentecostal magazine (the first of its kind), the *Christian Evangel*.

Myland encouraged them in the endeavor and wrote articles for the paper. He and J. Roswell also collaborated in the formation of the Association of Christian Assemblies in central Indiana. This group of Pentecostal congregations voluntarily joined forces to promote solid Bible teaching and evangelism. The first issue of the *Christian Evangel* in July of 1913 reported on the meeting. In addition to articles of news and teaching, both of which Flower held would testify to the Holy Spirit's work and encourage others to seek the Lord, the magazine carried a Sunday school lesson for children written by Alice Reynolds Flower. This was a first for Pentecostal publications; Pentecostals frequently ignored children and youth and some leaders even opposed Sunday schools. The Flowers's commitment to children and youth would be a hallmark of their long ministry.

THE FIRST GENERAL COUNCIL

Flower began reading other Pentecostal publications early in his Christian life. He corresponded with missionaries, evangelists, preachers, and workers, soliciting newsletters, testimonies, and reports from them to include at least portions of the writings in the *Pentecost* and the *Christian Evangel*. These various testimonies were a central part of his promotion of Pentecostal teaching and witness. As much as was being done by individuals and congregations, he knew so much more could be accomplished by cooperative efforts. That was a key reason for joining with Myland. At the same time, the desire to protect the autonomy of local assemblies was strong. His spirit and mind responded joyfully when he read the call for a meeting to discuss these issues at Hot Springs, Arkansas, published by E. N. Bell and others in *Word and Witness* late in 1913. Flower began making plans to attend the April 1914 gathering. He believed it would be a signal event. Little did he and Alice know how in the providence of God the trajectory of their lives was to be taken up into and set by that epoch-making council.

The Flowers laid careful plans for the publication and distribution of the *Christian Evangel* the month he would be in Arkansas. It would be a very busy month for Alice to add to being mother to one-year-old Joseph getting the magazine ready for publication each week and looking after the mission. Though not personally known to many of the Southern Pentecostal leaders, Flower was known through the editorship of his magazine. The assembled saints spent the first three days in corporate worship and prayer, unifying their hearts in the Lord. When they turned to business, the delegates elected E. N. Bell as temporary chairman and J. Roswell Flower as temporary secretary of the proceedings: Bell was forty-seven and a key leader among Pentecostals in the South; Flower was only twenty-five. He had lived in the American Midwest for about a dozen years but was still a Canadian citizen. His stenographic skills proved invaluable.

Before the participants, who represented several different groups, was the fivefold call for the convention, probably written by Bell: first, to resolve the divisions among them by coming to an agreed-upon body of biblical teaching to be held and preached in common; second, to conserve the work produced by evangelism; third, to have a better understanding of the needs of each foreign field; fourth, to charter churches using the same name for legal and business purposes; and, finally, to propose a general Bible training school with a literary department. This call became a pivotal document for Flower. He returned to it many times over the course of his long years of service to the Assemblies of God.

What the representatives did not have before them was an agreed upon definition of the "organization" they were to form. A formal committee was appointed to draft a statement about the nature of their relations. Numbers of men were so fearful that a binding legislative body would be created by that committee that they responded to T. K. Leonard's call for a clandestine committee to meet at night to produce a statement that would establish a unified, voluntary, cooperative fellowship in which the autonomy of local congregations was protected. Flower was the secretary of that committee, which met all night to hammer out its statement. The amazing similarity between the secret committee's and formal committee's reports was greeted with shouts of joy and praise for God's providential oversight to make known his will. The work of the two committees was combined into a "Preamble and Resolution of Constitution." This document was the second one that Flower repeatedly referenced along with the fivefold call for the Hot Springs convention that produced the General Council of the Assemblies of God. (See Appendix A.)

J. Roswell Flower

Another resolution of the council, linked to the call for it, addressed the need for both biblical education (Bible schools) and "literary" education, especially, though not exclusively, for children. The latter concern focused the need for literacy acquired in the context of faith and holy living. As public education in the United States expanded its reach and secularized its curriculum, many evangelical Christians became more concerned to have access to "Christian" education for their children. It was true that many Pentecostals touted their ignorance of academic learning as a badge of honor. However, both Bell and Flower argued that Christians needed substantial knowledge of the Bible and other subjects. Bell himself pursued undergraduate studies at Stetson University in Florida and graduate work at the Southern Baptist Seminary in Louisville, Kentucky and the University of Chicago Divinity School (then a Baptist institution) from which he graduated in 1903. He longed to study in Europe and sought to use his Stetson degree to be elected to one of the newly established Rhodes Scholarships at Oxford University, UK. He was ineligible, as it turned out, because he had pursued three years of study beyond his undergraduate degree. Even though his formal education occurred prior to his receiving the baptism of the Holy Spirit, Bell used the skills and knowledge he acquired to study Spirit-baptism carefully, to defend Trinitarianism against Oneness teaching, and to answer hundreds of questions sent to *Word and Witness* and the *Pentecostal Evangel*. J. Roswell Flower trusted and learned from Bell, eulogizing him later as "the sweetest, safest and sanest man I have ever met in Pentecost." Bell's impact on Flower, like that of Myland, was crucial.

CONCLUSION

At the end of the first council, Bell and Flower were elected as regular officers—chairman and secretary—of the new General Council of the Assemblies of God. They were no longer simply temporary officers for the duration of the convention. The meeting had proven to be epoch-making for them personally. Until his

Marriage and an Epoch Making Meeting

death in 1923, E. N. Bell would contribute his mature leadership to the fledgling Fellowship as chairman, editor, presbyter, and theological guide, a crowning achievement to a life of careful learning, spiritual growth, and compassionate action. J. Roswell Flower's spiritual life now had a "home" in which he would live, grow, and serve for more than five decades.

3

First Secretary of the General Council

Come, see how God is moving and preparing the saints for the rapture.
—J. ROSWELL FLOWER, *CHRISTIAN EVANGEL*, SEPTEMBER 12, 1914

E. N. BELL AND J. Roswell Flower lived in different places, Bell in Arkansas and Flower in Indiana. To facilitate the work of the new organization, T. K. Leonard offered the men and their families the opportunity to move to Findlay, Ohio where he operated a Bible school and owned printing equipment. The men would need to find housing for themselves and their families. However, the Bible school building with print shop could serve as the headquarters for the organization and as the publishing house for the magazines Bell and Flower edited. Both men gave their respective magazines to the General Council; Bell's monthly *Word and Witness* moved from Malvern, Arkansas and Flower's weekly *Christian Evangel* moved from Plainfield, Indiana. As chairman of the General Council, Bell became the managing editor of the papers; J. Roswell

First Secretary of the General Council

was the assistant managing editor. Later the two papers were combined into an enlarged weekly.

PROMOTING THE GENERAL COUNCIL

Before the Hot Springs council concluded, Flower telephoned a report to Alice on the first few days of the meeting. She wrote up the material for the *Christian Evangel* and had copies of the printed issue shipped down to her husband before the end of the inaugural sessions. When he returned to Indiana the last part of April, he published more about the meeting and the formation of the General Council of the Assemblies of God. He invited readers of the magazine to send him ten thousand names of those who were not subscribers so that he could send them a complimentary issue. He wanted to flood the mails with Pentecostal material; to do so would require that others also publish their news, testimonies, teachings, and so forth, and he challenged them to do so. When Bell returned to Malvern from Hot Springs, he published the "Preamble and Resolution on Constitution" and a report of the council in the May issue of *Word and Witness*. Once the office in Findlay was set up in July, 1914, the men published the minutes of the first General Council as prelude to the second Council scheduled for November.

The move to Ohio was difficult for the Flowers. J. Roswell was immediately busy getting the weekly magazine out on time. Furthermore, he helped Bell with the receipt and distribution of missionary funds sent to the General Council office. Even while they were still living in Indiana, Alice lamented the loneliness she experienced as her husband of necessity was busy. In Findlay she believed he was so busy that his spiritual life was suffering. Certainly their domestic happiness was affected. One of Alice's twin sisters, Zella, had moved with them to help at home with the care of Joseph (now a toddler) as well as to provide some office help. On one occasion the boy slipped out ("ran away") of the house unnoticed and was discovered more than a block away by a neighbor. Zella wrote to the family that the son takes after "his worthy father." Alice was comforted by a refreshing time of prayer with J. Roswell and her realization that the Lord's coming must be near.

Belief in the imminence of Christ's return to rapture the saints was a key doctrine in the fourfold gospel: Christ as Savior, as Baptizer in the Holy Spirit, as Healer of the body, and as soon-coming King. The outbreak of World War I in Europe in August of 1914 surely heralded that his coming was so near that nothing should be allowed to distract the saints from the work of the gospel. Many people were prophesying the coming of the Lord that year; others cited 1917 or even 1933 as the year of his appearing. Flower and Bell published notice of some of these prophetic messages in their papers; neither man held that they should be accepted as Scripture. They published them as a comfort and stimulus for believers to be diligent in their lives and service.

The war, even before US participation, raised a second, multi-layered question for Pentecostal believers, most especially for Europeans. How should one think about war? Should believers participate in war as combatants, possibly killing other human beings (even fellow Pentecostals!)? Should the General Council declare the fellowship pacifist and require members to avoid combat? Did the Bible require Christians to be pacifists? One European brother argued for the concept of a just war in which Pentecostals might participate. An American pastor and Bible school teacher argued for a pacifist position. Flower published both pieces in the *Christian Evangel*. He did not avoid the controversy. Rather, he insisted that the periodical should be the kind of paper that published key items of importance even if others disagreed with them. Flower himself countered the pacifist argument, which was based on Jesus' nonresistance to his capture and crucifixion, pointing to the uniqueness of Jesus' position. Christ was born to die. Therefore, his behavior should not be used to make an argument for national nonresistance. He stopped short of declaring his own position. However, the Council did not. They took a peace position, asserting both support and respect for the government of the United States of America and declaring the conviction that participation in war was contrary to the Christian faith. However, each member or adherent was left free to decide their belief and course of action.

THE SECOND GENERAL COUNCIL

Flower was deeply committed to the basic principles of the General Council: unity, voluntary cooperation, and fellowship. Pentecostals were fearful of creating an organization whose ruling executive body would have power to dictate unscriptural doctrines and practices for member assemblies, that is, to require belief and practice of some unscriptural doctrine(s) or practice(s) as a condition of fellowship. He believed that the Hot Springs meeting established protections against such a possibility in the "Preamble and Resolution on Constitution." What was protected was the freedom of local assemblies. The General Council, on the other hand, was protected from local ministers or churches promulgating unscriptural doctrines and practices in that it was given authority to identify what was "unscriptural" and to affirm what was "scriptural." Along with the announcement of the next General Council to be held in Chicago at the Stone Church in November, Flower urged all Pentecostals whether currently affiliated with the General Council of the Assemblies of God or not to come to the Chicago meeting to see and participate in the freedom and order balanced and harmonized in the organization. He also urged all those interested in attending the council to acquire and read a copy of the minutes of the April meeting. To that end, he and Bell published those minutes that all might understand what had been accomplished at Hot Springs.

Some decisions at the Council in Chicago had a direct impact on J. Roswell and his family. He was reelected as the general secretary. Thus, when the Council decided to move the headquarters and publishing house to St. Louis, Missouri in January 1915, Flower and family were faced with a move at the same time their second child was due. George and Bethia Flower, J. Roswell's parents, were still living in Indianapolis. They invited Alice to bring Joseph and come to their home for the birth of the baby and the

J. Roswell Flower

mother's recovery before the three of them would join J. Roswell in St. Louis. He was left to do the major packing up of their home and seeing to the removal of their belongings to a new residence. Alice wrote detailed instructions for him regarding many items, especially fragile ones. On the night of January 9, 1915 J. Roswell received a telegram from Alice's father (her parents lived a few miles north of the Flowers in Indianapolis), "Girl Came Eight Fifteen PM Both Doing Well Congratulations." She was named Alice Adele.

The move to St. Louis necessitated the purchase of printing equipment to be used exclusively for the General Council (GC). The primary work was the regular publication of the *Christian Evangel* (weekly) and *Word and Witness* (monthly). E. N. Bell remained as the managing editor of the magazines, but he was replaced as Chairman of the GC by Arch P. Collins. Flower continued as assistant managing editor. The move to Missouri also required changing the name of the *Christian Evangel*. There was already a magazine by that name in St. Louis. *Weekly Evangel* was chosen as the new name for the paper.

With his family back together and the recently acquired printing equipment installed at the plant in St. Louis, Flower turned his attention to a resolution that had been put forward at the November Council. Introduced by L. C. Hall and unanimously approved by the delegates, it committed the Assemblies of God and the Pentecostal movement to the "greatest evangelism the world has ever seen." Flower wrote that the resolution was part of the stirring up of believers to the task of evangelism for which the Holy Spirit had been poured out in latter rain. Already the fruit of that outpouring was evident in the spirit of unity, cooperation, and fellowship among the assemblies. These things were not to be taken for granted, however. Spiritual unity had a price tag, "persistent effort." He saw the fundamental principle in Genesis 11:6: "and now nothing will be restrained from them, which they have imagined to do." The people of Babel had come together to build a tower around which they would gather in opposition to God's command for them to spread out over the earth. If such united effort established power against the purposes of God, how much more would the unity of God's people in the Holy Spirit around the commitment to push forward world evangelization be empowered to succeed.

THE NEW ISSUE

The unity in which J. Roswell rejoiced in April of 1915 was shattered a few months later. Two years earlier a dispute had arisen in the movement over the baptismal formula. Pentecostals generally used the Trinitarian wording from Matthew 28:19. At a camp meeting in California in the summer of 1913, a Canadian minister emphasized the wording of Acts 2:38, "in the name of Jesus Christ." Subsequently, another man claimed he had a "revelation" affirming that baptism should be in the name of Jesus only. Flower noted in the *Christian Evangel* in the fall that the question had been settled in the third century AD when the church determined that the gospel formula should be used. He encouraged the study of church history to help Christians avoid misinterpreting the Bible. Nevertheless, the dispute had been growing and becoming more acrimonious as the debate passed beyond the baptismal formula to theology proper. Is God Triune or One? Some who came to believe that the Trinitarian concept of God was wrong also rejected the Matthew wording as a legitimate baptismal rite. Persons baptized with that formula needed to be rebaptized to be rightly related to God and to others who had been immersed "in the name of Jesus only." The three basic principles of the GC—unity, voluntary cooperation, and fellowship—were threatened.

The storm broke in the summer of 1915 when E. N. Bell, former chairman and then managing editor of the official magazines of the General Council, was rebaptized, setting off a veritable flood of rebaptisms in both the United States and Canada. Flower realized the fledgling organization could be destroyed by the upheaval. He cooperated with other presbyters to call a general council for October in St. Louis. At the council he was reelected as secretary; J. W. Welch replaced Arch P. Collins as chairman. The delegates discussed both the doctrine and practice involved in the "New Issue" and then called on all members to spend a year carefully studying the Scriptures addressing the questions. The leadership broadly recommended use of the Trinitarian baptismal wording, but did not legislate its use. They discouraged breaking fellowship with others based on the use of one or the other formulae.

The following year was a trying one for the Flowers. When J. W. Welch arrived in St. Louis to begin his term as Chairman of the General Council, he decided to have all the headquarters personnel move into a large building sectioned off into appropriately sized apartments. J. Roswell and Alice were expecting a third child, George Ernest, who was born in March 1916. Now the mother of three small children, Alice also continued to write Sunday school lessons for the *Weekly Evangel* and edit a devotional column for it. The rising price of paper caused by the War and the decision to merge the two official organs into a single sixteen-page weekly increased the stress on the magazine staff. The financial pressure became so severe J. Roswell suffered from hives. As the months slipped by and the 1916 Council date approached, the tensions between the two sides of the New Issue rose. Flower had steadfastly stood for the Trinitarian position and sided with the statement of the presbyters espousing it. He suffered the strains of the conflict.

In the summer of 1916 the Flowers decided to take a break by traveling across southern Missouri from east to west (from Cape Girardeau to Springfield) to visit various Bible camps, revivals, and churches. It was the first "rest" they had taken since beginning the *Christian Evangel* three years earlier. It is not clear that the trip overall produced much rest—they often ministered wherever they stopped. However, the first day did hold an extraordinary moment reminiscent of their shared experience of nature in Indianapolis several years earlier. They travelled from St. Louis to Cape Girardeau by boat down the Mississippi River under a rainy sky. Approaching their destination, they went out on the deck of the boat and saw to the west a sunset that filled the clearing sky with golden light from north to south like molten metal. Looking back east, they saw a brilliant double rainbow against the still-blackened sky.

It seemed as though God's promise to Noah was being renewed to them.

THE 1916 GENERAL COUNCIL

To forestall much unnecessary wrangling over the doctrinal questions at the council, a committee was appointed to draft a "Statement of Fundamental Truths" (SFT) with special attention given to the nature of the Godhead. E. N. Bell was on the committee, now once again securely taking a Trinitarian stance. The key figure was Daniel W. Kerr, college graduate, longtime Christian and Missionary Alliance and Pentecostal minister, and of scholarly temperament. Kerr spent months leading up to the October assembly pouring over his Greek New Testament and nineteenth-century studies on the Trinity. His voluminous notes and draft of the seventeen articles of the original SFT eased the discussions about and preparation of the final version. Some delegates objected that the General Council had declared at Hot Springs that the Bible alone was its standard of faith and practice and that no creed would be written. On the other hand, the Council had been given the authority to identify which doctrinal positions and ministry practices were scriptural and which unscriptural. Was the Statement of Fundamental Truths a creed or merely a delineation of the scriptural truth "essential to a full Gospel ministry," "a basis of unity for the ministry alone (i.e., that we all speak the same thing, 1 Cor 1:10; Acts 2:42)," as its opening statement declared?

Sufficient numbers of those gathered, including Flower, perceived the document as a clear presentation of doctrines they held to be consistent with Scripture so as to set the standard for the General Council. The long, detailed Article 13 on the Godhead affirmed only a Trinitarian position, thereby excluding Oneness teaching, marking it as unscriptural. The immediate impact of the approval of the SFT was the loss of about 27 percent of the ministers credentialed with the General Council; the number dropped from 585 to 429. However, Flower noted that within a few weeks following the decision many ministers and churches, even groups of churches, which had stood apart from the General Council because of the confusion over doctrine, began seeking to affiliate with the Assemblies of God. There was a clear standard around which to unify and engage in evangelism with confidence. The long-term result was solid growth. Subsequently, the renewal of pastoral credentials and all applications for new credentials required applicants to read the SFT carefully and to sign an affirmation of faith.

Though Flower never boasted about his own role in the New Issue controversy, it is clear that his steady hold on the church's historically orthodox position on the Godhead and his irenic leadership during the months of conflict and uncertainty contributed to preserving the Assemblies' story as a Fellowship within the historic Christian community. At the same time, he never charged that Oneness believers were not saved nor genuinely filled with the Holy Spirit. Years later he argued that they were wrong in their heads but right in their hearts. He was both a founding father of the Assemblies of God and a man of generous spirit.

CONCLUSION

To the strain of the startup years of the Flowers's weekly magazine and the General Council were added the extreme pressures of the Oneness conflict, the growth of their family, and their hectic life in St. Louis. The group home in which they lived was constantly called upon to welcome and host guests from far and near. During the 1916 GC, some forty additional people were housed in the home. J. Roswell decided to withdraw from the executive leadership of the Fellowship and from the office manager's position at the Gospel Publishing House. He did not stand for re-election at the Council. He and Alice needed time and space to reassess God's calling and leading in their lives and ministries.

4

Secretary of the Missionary Department

Pentecostal missionaries have a Pentecostal commission—to be witnesses in Jerusalem, in Judea, in Samaria and the uttermost parts of the earth. WITNESSES!

—J. ROSWELL FLOWER, "THE PENTECOSTAL COMMISSION"

EVANGELISM

FLOWER HAD SPENT MORE than three years as a magazine editor, officer in two Pentecostal organizations (the Association of Christian Assemblies and the General Council of the Assemblies of God), and office manager of the Gospel Publishing House. During that time he and Alice became the parents of three children and constantly faced financial needs for both themselves and the organizations they served. In the spring of 1917, he took his wife and the two smaller children to Gate, Oklahoma in the panhandle. His sister and her husband, Bernice and Frank Alexander, had purchased a farm there with two residences; the elder Flowers (George and Bethia) moved from Indianapolis to join them. Some weeks later Flower returned to Gate from St. Louis and noticed the striking differences in his family. He wrote to Alice's parents, Charles and Mary Alice Reynolds (with whom Joseph was staying), who had remained in Indianapolis, that the strain had gone from Alice's face and the children had lost their peakedness. Little Adele's cheeks looked like ripe strawberries which he constantly wanted to nibble. Alice was more relaxed, showing less of the strain and weariness she had in St. Louis. If, he continued, the family could remain in that kind of setting for a year, they would all be renewed and fortified for whatever the years ahead might hold. Flower revealed both his concern for his wife and family and a recognition that if Jesus Christ tarried his return they would have to learn how to pace their lives.

Apparently at a family council, they decided to move out of St. Louis. J. Roswell was dispatched from Gate to find a farm in Missouri suitable for both his family and his parents. He found a property at Stanton (near Sullivan), Missouri, about sixty miles southwest of St. Louis. By early fall both J. Roswell's family and his parents were on the farm, which they named "Maranatha" (see 1 Cor 16:22). For nearly ten years, Maranatha provided a place of retreat for J. Roswell and his growing family. A fourth child, Suzanne Grizelle, was born to them in November 1918. Having resigned from the Gospel Publishing House, J. Roswell was free from that pressure. However, what field of ministry he should pursue was not clear. Alice wrote her parents that she wanted him "to fill just God's place of service." That place of service turned out to be evangelism and Bible conference work with periodic calls from the publishing house for him to return and help.

Holding evangelistic meetings sometimes required Flower to be away from the family for a few days or more at a time. He and Alice deeply appreciated the presence of George and Bethia Flower. His father stepped in to conduct the family altar in the son's absence. The Flower children were receiving from their grandfather the spiritual nurture J. Roswell had as a child. Also, the elder

Secretary of the Missionary Department

Flowers were gardeners and outdoor people. As the children grew they gained a sense of nature and farm life that Alice believed was most important. It helped inure them to the vain social allure of urban life, she wrote to her parents.

The 1917 General Council approved the search for and purchase of property outside St. Louis to relocate the GC offices and the publishing house. When E. N. Bell discovered a suitable site in Springfield, Missouri, in the spring of 1918, Flower was asked to travel to Springfield to examine the property and negotiate its purchase. Having done so, he was then asked to help with moving the office and printing equipment from St. Louis and setting up the plant in Springfield. This he did, necessitating more time away from his family who remained at Maranatha.

J. Roswell continued to observe the Pentecostal movement, the world scene, and the conditions in America during these years. He believed World War I, which the US had entered in April 1917, was an end-time war; it was even possible that the rapture of the saints would occur during the conflict and essentially go unnoticed by the world. The vehemence of the European war was matched by the upheavals in America. J. Roswell was particularly struck by the intensity of the race riot in East St. Louis, Illinois in July 1917. Blacks and whites behaved toward each other with the same reported ferocity of the Germans in Belgium. The arguments of liberal clergy and intellectuals that human beings were getting better were obviously the pronouncements of "false shepherds," another sign of the soon coming of Christ, as was the violence in the world. The days of Noah are here, he concluded in a letter to the editor of a St. Louis newspaper. In light of these conditions, Christians must be filled with the Spirit. He argued in an article published in the *Weekly Evangel* that seeking and receiving the baptism in the Spirit and speaking in tongues once was not the same thing as being filled with the Spirit daily. The danger of those who were not filled with the Spirit was not being prepared for the rapture. What is most interesting is that he did not stop the article with this warning. Rather, he continued by asking whether the rapture would be pre-tribulation or mid-tribulation. One's answer to that question he said depends on the interpretation of 2 Thessalonians 2:8 ("And then shall that Wicked be revealed, whom the Lord shall consume with the spirit of his mouth, and shall destroy with the brightness of his coming"). Some held that the rapture would occur before the antichrist began his peaceful ascent to power, pre-tribulation. Others held that the rapture would occur just before the antichrist's violent takeover of the world, mid-tribulation. J. Roswell warned that since there was much room for speculation about this matter, dogmatism should be avoided.

SECRETARY OF THE MISSIONS DEPARTMENT

Flower was careful to attend and participate in each and every General Council. He loved the concept of the General Council and the principles on which it rested. It could only be effective if all ministers and lay delegates actively supported it. Broad participation alone could prevent it from becoming the province of a religious oligarchy, the executive officers. He, also, continued writing for the *Evangel*, which, following the move to Springfield, was renamed the *Pentecostal Evangel*. The magazine, he had written, belonged to the *Evangel*-family. It, too, must be protected from becoming the mouthpiece of the editors and executives only. The heart of the Fellowship was evangelism, at home and abroad. Unity and cooperation were for the sake of the proclamation of the gospel in the power of the Holy Spirit to affect the largest work of evangelism possible before the imminent return of the Lord Jesus Christ.

Missions had been a major dimension of J. Roswell's involvement in Pentecostalism since his conversion. Even before he received the baptism in the Holy Spirit, he served as the missionary secretary of a small assembly in Indianapolis. He collected and mailed to the missionaries supported by the church all funds submitted for them. He promoted missions in each of the magazines he started and edited; he always included the testimonies and prayer appeals of missionaries at home and abroad. As general secretary of the General Council, he assisted the Chairman (later

Secretary of the Missionary Department

Superintendent) in the distribution of funds sent to headquarters. As the Fellowship grew and the number of missionaries approved by the GC expanded, the task of handling the funds and other business for missions and missionaries increased. Finally, at the 1919 General Council the decision was taken to establish a Department of Missions with a full-time secretary-treasurer to keep track of missionaries and to get the support received at headquarters to them. J. Roswell was elected as the first Missionary Secretary of the Assemblies of God.

The position required the Flowers to move to Springfield, a great step of faith. Flower was given a job but not a salary. Members of the Council were encouraged to send some "extra" with their missionary offerings designated for the secretary-treasurer. He and Alice prayed, lived frugally, and worked hard. God provided. Early in the six years J. Roswell served as the secretary-treasurer and treasurer-only, he realized that the post-World War I world was changing dramatically and rapidly. Those shifts necessitated a number of key interrelated changes in missionary training, funding, and appointment. First, he argued that changes in the world's economy and governments, and the ways they monitored missionaries, required the General Council officers to have a greater degree of personal knowledge of each missionary or missionary candidate than had earlier been the case. The GC should not approve a person or couple for service simply because they applied or were recommended by someone. This outraged key regional leaders, especially those on the West coast. Flower argued that the best way to ensure such knowledge was to have every missionary applying for new credentials or renewal to visit headquarters in Springfield for several days. Better still, each candidate should spend one semester, or more, at a new institution, Central Bible Institute (CBI), in Springfield. Other educators were upset. They saw this as undermining their work and reducing the number of students who would attend their schools. And in some ways, it was so. Flower believed that CBI should be made into the premier educational institution for training missionaries who were to receive GC approval and appointment.

Second, the kind of training the school should provide needed to go far beyond standard Bible school training. Knowledge of the Bible, including biblical languages, and theology needed to be augmented by careful and thorough training in General Council of the Assemblies of God history, polity, and principles to reduce strife, conflict, and misrepresentation on the field. Missionaries should be trained in the language of the field they planned to serve as well as in world history and culture with special attention to the country or field to which the missionary was going. The early, widespread belief that God would give missionaries the language of their country supernaturally had resulted in many disasters on the field. Missionaries must settle into the hard work of language learning, understanding historical and cultural contexts, and becoming acquainted with traditions, customs, and religions of their language group. Flower argued that CBI should be made into that kind of school located in Springfield where each candidate would be known to the Missionary Department leaders.

Third, Flower grew increasingly concerned about the funding of approved missionaries. Some, he observed, were receiving more funds than they needed while others were nearly destitute. One of the goals of the founding of the GC at Hot Springs was to have greater knowledge of the needs of missionaries and see that each field and person was adequately supplied. Flower knew that half to three quarters of all missionary giving was sent directly to the field from an individual donor or assembly. Furthermore, many funds sent to headquarters were designated for a missionary. Only a relatively small amount of support was undesignated. How could the secretary-treasurer possibly distribute funds fairly if he did not know how much a missionary needed and was already receiving? Given rising costs worldwide, and rapid increases in some areas, Flower suggested that fifty dollars per person a month was necessary for most fields. Some would require more. If all funds were sent to the Missionary Department, an equitable distribution could be made.

Flower's suggestions and proposals smacked of a dreaded "centralization" of authority and were rejected by the Council. He

Secretary of the Missionary Department

was made the treasurer-only. Despite the change in his position, the Flowers remained in Springfield. Two more sons were born to them, Roswell Stanley (Rossie) and David Warren. J. Roswell and Alice and their family of six continued to host missionary families passing through the city or in the city on business. Often, the children slept on palettes on the floor, giving up their beds to the missionaries. Feeding their guests stretched the resources of the Flowers very thin on more than one occasion. Both husband and wife remained active in ministry at Central Assembly of God; some of their days during revival services began early in the morning and lasted until midnight. Nonetheless, J. Roswell believed that the national office should be a good neighbor and municipal citizen. He took time and sought to make friends or at least acquaintances of the merchants along Commercial Street a block north of the headquarters' building. It was a policy he pursued to the end of his active career.

The General Council of 1925 decided to combine all treasury functions into a general treasurer post. Flower thought such a position should be held by a businessman. He declined to stand for election for the office, resigning from headquarters. Wanting to be more active in direct ministry, he accepted the pastorate of the Scranton Pentecostal Church, Scranton, Pennsylvania.

CONCLUSION

During the decade between 1914 and 1925, J. Roswell served the General Council of the Assemblies of God as its first general secretary, as an editor of the official magazine, office manager for the Gospel Publishing House, and the first Missionary Department secretary-treasurer. He was only twenty-five at the Hot Springs convention; he was now thirty-seven. Financial pressures both at home and at work, difficult decisions about doctrines and practices in the Fellowship, and concerns for a growing family had all been his lot. Approaching forty, Flower was beginning a pastoral ministry far from the cultural environment of the relatively homogenous Midwest of Indiana, Ohio, and Missouri in which he

J. Roswell Flower

had come of age. In fact, Alice was uncertain about the move, but willing to trust God that her husband's decision was the right one. And so, in mid-December the family started driving east, arriving in Scranton on New Year's Day of 1926. Joseph, who was twelve, remained in Springfield with Alice's father C. E. Reynolds and her sister Ulela Reynolds to complete the school year. Pennsylvania would be their home for the next decade and the Eastern District their field of service.

5

The Eastern District Decade
Pastor and Superintendent

[B]egin now to teach your people the truth of God on the subject of the gifts and ministries of the Spirit, so that when the need comes, they will be prepared to withstand the error. Prevention is better than cure.

—J. ROSWELL FLOWER, "BEWARE OF FALSE PROPHECY"

THE FLOWERS'S TEN-YEAR MINISTRY in the Eastern District was divided into two periods. The first four years were spent in Scranton as pastor of the Pentecostal Assembly. The last six years, during the time J. Roswell was District Superintendent, the family lived in Lititz, Pennsylvania. In addition to the long road trip from Springfield east across the Midwestern states, through the mountains of western Pennsylvania, and into the Lackawanna Valley in the northeastern part of the state, Alice was uncertain about the very different cultural, religious, and economic contexts of the coal country of Pennsylvania. Furthermore, she was concerned about the public schools in the city, especially, the high school for Joseph.

Many years later, however, she could write in her memoirs of the family that the decision to move was clearly the Lord's leading.

SCRANTON, 1926–1930

The population of the region was made up of several European ethnic groups, some of which were predominantly Roman Catholic. Many of the people were first and second generation immigrants. The assembly at Scranton had ten or eleven different ethnic groups and several members were from a Catholic background. The Flowers were encouraged by the warm and helpful welcome the church gave them on that New Year's Day when they arrived in the city.

The spiritually vibrant church in Scranton was founded a few years prior to the organization of the General Council of the Assemblies of God. In 1914 the church moved into its Scranton location from a small town north of the city, hired its first fulltime pastor, David H. McDowell, and joined the newly established Fellowship. McDowell later became an assistant general superintendent and moved to Springfield, Missouri, while Flower was still the Missionary Treasurer. Two years later the man who replaced McDowell in Scranton resigned due to ill health, the same year Flower stepped away from national office and accepted the call to the assembly.

As early as 1908, Flower's nascent pastoral heart was evident. He discerned quickly the needs of the congregations in central Indiana where he and two other young men were holding meetings. Later when he was preaching in other towns in Indiana and other states, he gauged what the people could digest spiritually and taught them accordingly. He did the same thing in Scranton. He rejoiced at the healthy life of the church but saw they lacked solid biblical and theological teaching beyond the practical matters of Christian life and worship. Without neglecting evangelistic services and protracted meetings, he carefully taught basic systematic theology through sermons. He also taught adult Bible studies, encouraging the reading of Scripture beyond a devotional level. Doing this kind of teaching required him to continue reading

The Eastern District Decade

and studying the Bible as well as church history and theology. He saturated all his study in prayer and saw the fruit of his study and prayers in conversions, healings, and the growth of individual believers as they sought and received the baptism in the Holy Spirit.

Contrary to many Pentecostal leaders who gave little thought to the needs of children and youth, J. Roswell and Alice had been attentive to them since their early days in Indianapolis. While he focused primarily on the adults in the congregation, Alice worked hard for the younger members of the flock. They began a Christ's Ambassadors program for the young people at the church, the first one in the eastern part of the United States. They had some services for the youth especially; but, these were never at the same time as the adult meetings. Instead, the young people were encouraged to participate in the adult services not only by attendance; the Flowers also taught them how to receive the baptism in the Holy Spirit, how to be prayer warriors for the services and ministries of the assembly, and, for the older ones, how to discern their spiritual gifts and minister them in appropriate ways in the regular services. This is the way they themselves had learned from first generation leaders such as Thomas Hezmalhalch and D. Wesley Myland in Indianapolis.

J. Roswell had learned the value of summer Bible camps for evangelism and teaching within two years of his conversion. Camps offered opportunities for periods of intense teaching and discipleship training. He rejoiced at the Eastern District's extensive use of the camps, becoming very active in them from the first summer he and his family arrived there. The district was large, covering Pennsylvania, New York, New Jersey, and Delaware. Not owning its own campgrounds, the district annually held two or three regional camps at rented facilities. The Flowers's active participation in the various functions of the district soon made leaders and pastors aware of J. Roswell's gifts and anointing for teaching and leadership. He had already taught classes at T. K. Leonard's Bible school in Findlay, Ohio in the first bloom of the Fellowship and at Central Bible Institute in Springfield, Missouri when it began in 1922. In 1927 he was elected to the executive committee of the district leadership as secretary. Bethel Bible Training School in Newark, New Jersey tapped him as a part-time faculty member. He drove from Scranton to Newark each Thursday and returned Friday night. In a diary entry his daughter Adele remarked about the joy of the children when he arrived home. All of these activities were time-consuming. Alice wrote to her father and sister that each additional demand on her husband's time increased her responsibilities at home and at the Scranton assembly.

There were other pressures on the family as well. Flower was becoming well known in both the community of Scranton as well as among other ministers. Alice wrote that many Catholic folks thought of J. Roswell as a "priest" and consulted him. People came to the house to be married, to receive counselling, and to seek guidance, even other ministers from the larger mainline churches and secular leaders. The Flowers became friends with David Kins, the pastor of the African Methodist Episcopal Church (AME). He received the baptism in the Holy Spirit and sometimes came to the Scranton church for worship and spiritual refreshing. On one occasion the AME congregation hosted a woman evangelist for a revival. The Flowers and some members of the Scranton Assembly attended; J. Roswell stayed each night to pray with seekers at the altars, sometimes until past midnight. During these years the children were becoming more active in school affairs, scouting, music lessons, and youth activities in the District. The balance for their busy lives was the daily family prayer time, a practice begun on the Flowers's wedding night and continued. This daily event, conducted immediately following the evening meal, oriented their lives individually and collectively toward God and each other as well as all outside events.

LITITZ, 1930–1936

At the District Council in January 1930, Flower was elected as the Superintendent of the Eastern District. He was given no salary; free will offerings were to be his income. There was no office or residence for the district and his election did not require the family to relocate. However, he and Alice did not think it wise to remain in Scranton when the assembly hired a new pastor. They decided to remain in the city until the end of the school year in June. Joseph was a senior, set to graduate from high school. Adele and George were in high school also and involved in various activities. The younger children, Suzanne and Rossie (David was not yet in school), were happy in Scranton. The decision gave the adults time to determine criteria for selecting a new residence. They chose Lititz. The moral quality of the city was high. Founded by Nicolas Count von Zinzendorf, it was predominantly populated and controlled by Moravian Brethren. There was no Pentecostal church in the city, although Lancaster a few miles away had a thriving assembly. The lack of any existing Pentecostal church made Lititz "neutral" for the District Superintendent. The city boasted a good school system for the five younger children. Nearby Lancaster was also home to Franklin and Marshall College. J. Roswell and Alice wanted Joe to attend college but could not afford to send him to their first choice, Central Bible Institute in Springfield, Missouri. Finally, Lititz was more centrally located to the large population centers of the district, Philadelphia and New York City. They found a suitable residence and moved to the city in July of 1930.

J. Roswell did not exchange his pastoral heart for an administrative one when he assumed the office of District Superintendent in April. He merely changed his parish from Scranton Assembly to the ministers of the Eastern District. Furthermore, he brought to the position a cherished belief in the principles of the General Council as applicable to districts. Unity, voluntary cooperation, and fellowship were as practicable at that level as they were at the national level. When many people objected to the formation of district councils shortly after the General Council was formed in 1914, Flower argued that they were simply extensions of the GC's principles. At all levels these key concepts stimulated evangelism and disciple-making. Combined with the solid theological foundation of the Statement of Fundamental Truths, Flower trusted that the Assemblies of God would not experience the decline that most past revival movements had.

J. Roswell Flower

J. Roswell taught the ministers of the district something he had practiced in Scranton; visit each family in the congregation at least once a year. Some families might need more than one visit. He urged this in sermons and council sessions and tried to put it into practice. The size of the Eastern District made it nearly impossible to visit each minister at least once a year, but he made a herculean effort to do so. He drove hundreds of miles per week many times a year as the Great Depression deepened. Often his travel expenses left only a few dollars from offerings to add to the family budget. They suffered with most other ministers in the district the financial straits of the economic condition of the United States. Nonetheless, his visits were crucial in large and small ways. For one young minister in New York State who had been asked by the local high school to deliver the graduation address, J. Roswell outlined two possible talks, suggesting details. The man chose one of the talks and gave it almost exactly as his district superintendent had sketched it. The address was warmly received.

On another occasion, J. Roswell and Alice had gone to the assembly at New Kensington, Pennsylvania, for a Sunday morning service. The nineteen-month-old daughter of the pastor and his wife had been diagnosed with stomach flu. However, she was getting worse by the hour. The Flowers told the pastor to stay home with his wife and child while they took care of the service. Afterward, they went to the parsonage and found the situation becoming increasingly desperate. Undoubtedly, they recalled the critical illness of their three-year-old David a few years earlier in Scranton. They prayed fervently all night long for God to heal him of a disease that had claimed the lives of other children in the city. He and Alice gave themselves to prayer for the little girl as they had for David and God heard their prayers for her as he had for David. She was healed. Many years later during a surgery doctors found that the toddler's appendix had burst and were astounded that she had lived. She told them the story of how God had healed her in response to prayer.

Unity, cooperation, and fellowship were not possible without communication. Within three months of assuming the

The Eastern District Decade

Superintendent's office, Flower began a regular newsletter to inform the ministers of events at churches, camps, and in towns without churches. He solicited revival announcements, camp plans, tent meeting campaigns, prayer conferences, and other activities—musical, youth, vacation Bible school. He believed it was important that as many leaders as possible knew the goings-on in the district. Also, the newsletter gave him a vehicle for teaching and admonition. When a cult-like Pentecostal group from England moved into the District, he wrote to the ministers warning them of the "false prophets." He acknowledged his conviction that in general they were saved and that their Spirit-baptism was genuine. However, they interpreted the gift of prophecy in such a way that allowed them to take over and dominate existing assemblies. They did not start new churches; otherwise he would not have quarreled with them, he wrote. But they were destroying healthy AG congregations. He followed his warning with an urgent plea for the ministers to teach their people carefully and fully about the baptism in the Holy Spirit and the proper exercise of the gifts of the Spirit. He recommended they acquire and read Donald Gee's writings, especially *Concerning Spiritual Gifts*. A properly taught assembly would be forewarned and enabled to distinguish truth from error.

The Eastern District had two especially important needs that J. Roswell sought to meet: a permanent, district-owned campground and a Bible school affiliated with the General Council. Summer Bible camps continued to be a very important part of the spiritual life of the churches. As the Great Depression increased, worldliness increased also. Flower argued that times of worship, teaching, and revival in the context of a resident summer camp were a crucial stay against backsliding and spiritual decline. He and others had been looking for property that would be suitable for a permanent encampment. In early 1930, he found a forty-seven acre plot at Green Lane, Pennsylvania, near Philadelphia, that was superb. With his small son, David, he stood on the land and, praying fervently, claimed it for God and the Eastern District. The district acquired the property at a good price and despite the limitations of the times began building cabins, kitchens, and dining rooms and drilling wells. Many people raised their eyebrows and wondered about Flower when he moved ahead three years later with construction of a two-story, three-thousand-seat tabernacle with classrooms and some dormitory space. It was not only a question of money; but also, "Why build such an imposing edifice when Jesus is coming soon?" His answer to both questions was that God led them to build. The camp was a success in every way from the first summer sessions in August 1931 forward. The first service in that building was a youth rally with well over a thousand young people present!

The need for a Bible school linked to the General Council was the consequence of the closing of Bethel Bible Training School in the late 1920s. Bethel merged with Central Bible Institute in Springfield, Missouri, leaving the Eastern District without a school. The District Council decided to establish a Summer Bible Training School to meet on the campgrounds at Green Lane from Decoration (Memorial) Day to Labor Day beginning in 1932. J. Roswell was the titular head of the school and sometime teacher when his schedule as District Superintendent permitted. Alice became the functional head of the school for a few summers until Pastor Allen A. Swift came alongside to help and became principal when the Flowers returned to Springfield in the summer of 1936. The school's first year was so successful that the students asked that a second-year program be added the following summer. It was. The school filled a need so completely that it continued to flourish in the twenty-first century as the University of Valley Forge located in Phoenixville, Pennsylvania.

Flower knew that the General Council of the Assemblies of God only worked as it was designed to work when the district officers and pastors fully participated in the biennial meetings along with lay delegates from the assemblies. He himself continued to attend each Council. He spent weeks in 1931 driving to and from San Francisco, California where he was elected a non-resident assistant general superintendent. He was not required to move to Springfield, but did travel to executive meetings during the two years between Councils. He was re-elected in 1933. He could see that the older members of the first generation, such as E. N. Bell, J. W. Welch, and others, were passing on to their eternal reward. The members of the slightly younger generation, who were at Hot Springs, like himself, had now reached middle-age; many pulpits, especially in smaller towns and at newer churches, were being filled by men and women in their twenties and thirties. The imperative task was to pass on the essence of Pentecostal faith and practice to the new generation while guiding the movement into maturity without decline. Example and careful teaching were necessary.

Flower taught patiently, persistently, at every opportunity. He preached on the Holy Spirit frequently at conferences, meetings, and other opportunities. He taught pastors how to study, how to organize their time and order their priorities. He explained to them the need to reserve daily time for prayer and Bible reading and study as well as the importance of making a weekly schedule for visitation and other pastoral duties. He did not shy away from warning them of the dangers of sexual temptation, which required them to stay alert. He cited a text from the apocryphal book of Ecclesiasticus (Wisdom of Sirach) 2:1, "If thou my son consent to serve the Lord prepare thy soul for temptation," to underscore the dangers facing ministers. For those without Bible school training, he urged them to attend Central Bible Institute in Springfield if at all possible. One aspect of the call to the first General Council focused on the need for Bible schools and a literary school. Not infrequently, Flower reminded the saints that, contrary to many who claimed ignorance as godliness, education was a lifelong task. He also emphasized the need for rest and relaxation. He himself loved photography, even had his own dark room when that was possible, and he built radios, usually crystal ones. He also enjoyed listening to mystery dramas on the radio as well as news, sports, classical music, and religious broadcasts as his time allowed. He read and re-read one of his favorite books apart from the Bible, John Bunyan's *Pilgrim's Progress*. Years later he made sure his grandchildren had copies of the book.

J. Roswell Flower

The exceedingly heavy schedule he had to keep; the constant financial pressure under which he and his family lived; and the completion of his initial goals as superintendent were among the reasons J. Roswell cited in a letter of resignation sent to the Eastern District of the Assemblies of God executive and credential committees in the spring of 1935. He requested that he not be considered for the superintendency at the next District Council. Furthermore, he had suffered from health problems for the past year; his energy level was very low, making every aspect of ministry difficult. He had no new vision for the District; nor did he have specific personal plans beyond finishing his term of office.

The combined summer camp and Maranatha Park Summer Bible School at the Green Lane campgrounds was a high point for participants in 1935. It was with the richness of the spiritual refreshing of the summer that J. Roswell, Alice, and some of the children headed to Dallas, Texas via Springfield, Missouri for the General Council late in the summer. J. Roswell was slated to preach at the opening service. He chose as his topic, "Back to Calvary," later published in the *Pentecostal Evangel*.

Taking 1 Corinthians 1:18, 23–24 as his text, Flower noted that Paul rejoiced that the Corinthian church had and exercised the full panoply of spiritual gifts, including tongues. Yet, the majority of the letter was the Apostle's calling the assembly to repent of sexual immorality, eating foods sacrificed to idols, misinterpreting the resurrection, and disorder in family and church life. How could that be? The answer, Flower asserted, was Paul's charge that the saints had neglected the cross, Calvary. The apostle called them back to the cross. Turning from an explication of the text to an application of it to the Assemblies of God Fellowship, J. Roswell noted the research of an unnamed scholar that religious movements tended to peak about twenty-five years from their inception and then begin to decline. It happened to the group the scholar represented. Did it have to happen to the AG, then slightly more than twenty-one years since its birth? Acknowledging his felt need for such a renewal of the experience of Calvary that he observed in the early days of Pentecost, he encouraged all to embrace the cross afresh to ensure that decline not be the story of the Assemblies of God. (See Appendix B.)

Following his opening sermon, Flower was re-elected for a third term as non-resident assistant general superintendent. Later, he was elected as general secretary, the post he had held from 1914 to 1916. When the Council was unable to settle on a person to fill the assistant general superintendent position, Flower was given leave to serve in both offices for one term. Election to the general secretary's office did require the Flowers to move back to Springfield after a decade in the east.

CONCLUSION

The ten years the Flowers spent in Pennsylvania were filled with rich opportunities for service at multiple levels: local pastors, Bible school teachers, district secretary, district superintendent, and founders of a summer Bible school that developed into a flourishing Bible college, and now a Christian university. He and Alice also changed in many ways. J. Roswell became a naturalized American citizen in 1934. In 1935 Alice regained her US citizenship, which she had lost on a technicality when she married her husband in 1911. They passed from young adulthood into the prime, mature years of middle age. And, for their future calling, they had become familiar with a much larger world than the American Midwest. It was an urbanized, metropolitan one that included the second largest city in the world (New York—soon to be the largest), a key city in American history (Philadelphia), and a diverse population reflecting many cultures and varieties of Christianity and speaking many languages. They saw up close the American "melting pot." In mind and spirit J. Roswell had grown deeper in Christ and the knowledge of his Word and Spirit, and his (Flower's) grasp of the larger world in which the General Council of the Assemblies of God was now making its way had expanded greatly.

6

Return to National Office

> We ... learned long ago to adjust ourselves to the providential leadings of the Lord, and to bow our heads to His precious will.
>
> —J. Roswell Flower, "A Farewell Word from the District Superintendent"

THE NEWS OF J. Roswell's election as General Secretary of the General Council reached the east long before he and his family were able to return from Dallas. Letters of congratulations poured in, most included lamentation of the loss sustained by the pastors of the Eastern District. And well they might. Springfield was already populated with able men from the Eastern District: Ernest S. Williams, W. I. Evans, J. R. Evans, Noel Perkin, and Ralph Riggs had all left the district to take up positions in headquarters or at Central Bible Institute. Flower's encouragement to the ministers of the district to rejoice in the leadership they provided for the national Fellowship must have been cold comfort now that his name was being added to the list. However, Flower had a greater commendation for the district. They were the largest missionary-giving district in the nation for the previous fiscal year. Just under

$57,000 of the national total of $269,960 (21 percent) had been given by the Eastern District. This incredible giving had been achieved even as the Great Depression persisted and they had built the wonderful campground facilities at Maranatha Park and sustained the Summer Bible School! Flower did not say so, but the giving reflected his long-standing love for and promotion of missions, and for the emphasis he and Alice placed on solid education as well as nurturing the spiritual life of the district. Many letters they received emphasized the growth of the spiritual, intellectual, organizational, and ecclesial life of the district during J. Roswell's administration.

J. Roswell was not a lame-duck superintendent. He had not been since submitting his request in April to step away from the office, and he was not when he returned from Dallas. For the final months of his term, he worked even harder, maintaining an incredible pace of travel and ministry. Finally, at Christmas time he had a few days of rest with his family in Lititz. The District Council and Prayer Conference were already scheduled for the early days of January 1936. Flower requested from the General Superintendent, Ernest S. Williams, permission to remain in the east until after the closing of these events on January 10 instead of being on the job in Springfield on January 2. Williams granted his request.

SPRINGFIELD, EXPANDING MINISTRY

Much had happened to the Flower family in the decade since they had moved to the east from Springfield. The four older children had all graduated from high school: Joseph attended Franklin and Marshall College for two years until finances were provided for him to attend CBI. He graduated from there and was ministering in New York State. Adele and Suzanne were both attending CBI. Money was so tight they were not able to come home for the Christmas holidays in 1935. George was living at home attending a state teacher's college near Lititz. Rossie and David were still in school, as was Frances, a boy Rossie's age who had come to live with the Flowers just before they moved from Scranton to Lititz. J.

J. Roswell Flower

Roswell and Alice decided that she and the boys would remain in Pennsylvania until the end of the school year in June of 1936. By contrast to the growth in their nuclear family, both of their fathers had died; only J. Roswell's mother remained of their parents.

The General Council had also grown. There were more churches in more places in the nation, more missionaries serving in more areas of the world, and the social status of the Assemblies of God was changing. As General Secretary, Flower wrote in reply to the inquiry of the mayor of one Alabama town explaining that the AG was not a cult. If the town permitted the congregation to build there, the assembly would be reputable and a good neighbor in the city. J. Roswell had demonstrated a capacity for growth and change as a leader even as he steadfastly espoused and taught the fundamental doctrines and practices of the Fellowship and adhered to the principles of the General Council. He was alert to the changes in the nation and the world and was unusually perceptive of what these changes meant for the church.

Flower had been a member of the executive committee since being elected as assistant general superintendent at the 1931 General Council and re-elected in 1933. He regularly traveled to Springfield to attend committee meetings; he knew the men with whom he had to work. However, his working relationship to them changed both by position and residency. As the previous general secretary became less able to carry out his duties, the other executives picked up some of the load. Flower had to learn what his job actually entailed. Even three weeks after his arrival at headquarters, he wrote Alice that he still had not been told what he was expected to do. Some things he was sure were in his portfolio were being done by others. He supposed he would just have to "horn in" in order to establish the parameters of his duties. That would come in time, he told his wife. This was among the many things he wrote her in long newsy letters over the six months they were separated.

An item of first importance on his personal agenda was to find a residence suitable for the family. After looking at a number of different houses, he found a two-story place within easy walking distance of headquarters, then at the corner of Pacific and Lyon

Streets. He sketched the floor plans of both stories in a letter to Alice, describing the house, the lot, and the neighborhood, including some of the neighbors. When she agreed to the place, he began preparing it for them evenings and Saturdays when he was in town—repapering walls, painting some rooms and the woodwork, and scrubbing floors. Adele and Suzanne sometimes took time away from their studies at CBI and social events to help him. Adele had a part-time job at headquarters a few afternoons of the week, so she saw her father more often than Suzanne did. She wrote her mother that Daddy missed her greatly. She and Suzanne tried to cheer him up, but were only partially successful. He repeatedly wrote of longing for the time the family would be back together. The girls also helped him select which rooms would work best for different family members, decide what furniture they already had that was suitable to move from Pennsylvania, and search for other needed items in Springfield. By late June, family members, including Queenie the family dog, were all in Springfield, except for Joseph, who was pastoring in New York State, and George, who remained in Lancaster, Pennsylvania to complete his education at Millersville State Teachers College. Frances moved with them and remained a part of the family until he graduated from high school. J. Roswell and Alice, with the younger children, all joined Central Assembly of God, where they had been so much a part of the congregation before leaving the city ten years earlier.

Several avenues of ministry opened to Flower because of his position and the gifts God had given him. Together, he and Alice began a Sunday school class at Central in about 1937. J. Roswell presented the background of, the biblical content of, and theological reflections on the lesson; Alice applied it to the practical and daily life-situations of the members. This class continued into the twenty-first century under the subsequent leadership of their sons Joseph R. and David W. Also, J. Roswell and Alice both had more time for writing as a form of ministry. J. Roswell had produced thousands of pages of sermon notes, reports, news articles, and letters; however, his travel schedule in the east worked against him being able to write the sustained and thoughtful articles he considered. He now had time to work on more substantial writings. Behind him were nearly thirty years of a rich and varied Pentecostal ministry and a lifelong habit of reading, listening to, and engaging with a wide range of religious and secular people, books, papers, magazines, radio programs, and public addresses. At nearly fifty he had the maturity of mind and spirit and the energy of his prime to produce a substantial body of practical theology. The office of General Secretary brought Flower many invitations to preach and teach in varied settings—churches, summer camps, district councils, school and college assemblies, graduations, etc., as well as ecclesiastic and civic meetings. He was interviewed by newspapers and magazines; invitations to write for public interest periodicals gave him opportunity to explore the significance, impact, and role of the Assemblies of God as an organization. Whatever the particular venue or audience, J. Roswell never lost sight of the purpose for which God had called and positioned him, to make Christ known in an appropriate way. Furthermore, he never lost his pastoral heart.

SOME KEY WRITINGS

J. Roswell's first and foremost concern was the life of God in the General Council of the Assemblies of God at three levels: individuals, local assemblies, and the Fellowship at large. All three were in focus in an August 1936 *Pentecostal Evangel* article, "The Outstanding Effect of the Pentecostal Baptism." Phrased as a question, "What is the outstanding effect of the baptism in the Holy Spirit?," Flower's answer was immediate, "Spiritual utterance, inspired utterance." In the Old Testament the Spirit-empowered ministries of Elijah and Elisha were manifested primarily in the working of signs and wonders. However, the vast majority of the OT prophets from Isaiah to Malachi were speaking/writing ones. Without denigrating the importance of miracles as part of the Pentecostal outpouring in Jerusalem, Topeka, and Los Angeles, Flower noted that the common, surprisingly primary manifestation was speaking in other tongues "as the Spirit gave them utterance" and prophecy, in other words, empowered speech. He carefully distinguished the revelatory, inscripturated prophecies of the OT prophets from the New Testament gift of prophecy, calling the latter "inspirational speaking" not to be confounded with revelation or with prepared preaching and teaching. The evidence of an individual receiving the baptism in the Holy Spirit was speaking in tongues; the evidence of a Spirit-filled assembly was the presence of "inspired utterances." These things being true, Flower argued that the absence (or significant decline) of Spirit-produced speech in the life of a congregation were sure signs of "spiritual paralysis and approaching death." If this situation prevailed widely in the Fellowship, it obviously was indicative of an unhealthy spiritual condition. To stay healthy, assemblies needed expression of the full range of inspired utterances given by the Holy Spirit: tongues, interpretation of tongues, prophecy, exhortation, teaching, intercession, and singing in the Spirit. What Flower insisted on was that these expressions were the extemporaneous exercises of the Holy Spirit's presence and the people's surrender to him.

In August of 1938, Flower and Noel Perkin (Missionary Secretary) were sent to Africa to examine the situations of Assemblies of God missionaries and the condition of their stations. When they arrived in Egypt, they took a weeklong side-trip to Palestine and then returned to Egypt before flying to Uganda. J. Roswell was asked to preach in Egypt. He wrote Alice that he chose to speak on "Be Filled with the Spirit." He had published a brief article with the same title in 1917. As was frequently the case, he later turned the sermon into a longer article, which was published in the *Pentecostal Evangel* in 1939 as "One Great Christian Essential: 'Be Filled with the Spirit'" (see Appendix C). The article was in significant measure a sequel to "The Outstanding Effect of the Pentecostal Baptism." Taking his text from Ephesians 5:18, Flower observed that many Pentecostals were taking a position with regard to Spirit-baptism not unlike some evangelicals were taking toward salvation. Whereas evangelicals were teaching "once saved, always saved," Pentecostals were implying "once baptized in the Spirit, always baptized in the Spirit." Flower argued that this attitude confused an act in the past with a current state. Being filled with the Spirit required a continual openness to the Holy Spirit's actions in one's soul. If persons ceased to be open to his divine operations, decline would mark their individual and collective lives. A significant way this decline would manifest itself was the absence of inspired speech. He specifically identified the lack of thanksgiving and exercise of tongues in private and the operation of tongues and interpretation and prophecy in the assembly as indications of loss. The only means of restoration was repentance. In the absence of repentance, people would begin to downplay the initial experience of Spirit-baptism itself. Minimizing or ceasing to advocate the baptism in the Holy Spirit undermined the distinct identity of the Assemblies of God and removed its reason for existing as a religious organization.

Besides the sermon/article, two other important things came out of the trip to Africa. One was the deep bond of friendship that developed between Flower and Perkin. The latter had become Missionary Secretary in the late 1920s and was reelected every subsequent General Council until his retirement the same year as J. Roswell's, December 1959. Flower, too, was reelected to his office each Council from 1935 to his retirement. The two men were the only ones to remain in executive office through those overlapping twenty-four years; all the other offices changed hands several times. The second thing was the transformation of Flower. He turned fifty in June of 1938. Though he had traveled widely within the United States (then, of course, comprised of only the forty-eight contiguous states), he had not been outside North America. When the decision was made to send the two men to Africa, Flower was at the District Council of Northern California. He had to rush home to Springfield so he and Perkin could be in New York to sail on an Italian liner bound for Alexandria, Egypt, via Italy. Two weeks after leaving California, he was in North Africa marveling at the rapidity of his trip. It made his head spin.

The ship was a microcosm of Europeans, with some Middle Easterners. One of their cabin-mates was the son of an Arab chieftain who condemned the British for their role in promoting Jewish

Return to National Office

settlements in Palestine and rejecting Arab control of the area. He was anxious for the brewing European war to commence so the Arabs could rise up against the British and expel them from the region. Flower and Perkin saw the Italian preparations for war during the brief layover in an Italian port before sailing on to Alexandria. J. Roswell could not resist surreptitiously taking a few prohibited pictures in Italy. From Egypt, they spent several days in Palestine, becoming aware of the complex difficulties in that region. Returning to Alexandria they flew to Uganda. Over the next several weeks they journeyed westward to Liberia by air, riverboat, truck, bus, car, and hammock across the northern tier of European colonies in Sub-Saharan Africa. Flower sent home dozens of letters written in very small cursive script detailing their movements, experiences, sights, sounds, smells, environments, people, church services, meals, flora, and fauna—everything. He preached to doctors, lawyers, and socialites on the ship. He saw the power of God at work among people who still wore nothing but loin clothes in the bush in Africa. On the return trip they sailed to London and visited Noel Perkin's brother before sailing from England back to New York. The trip prepared him for the extensive international travel and ministry he engaged in after the Second World War. It contributed to a deepening of his insights into humanity's religious longings and their expressions. He saw ever more clearly the need for, the power of, and the beauty of the gospel as God's answer to human need.

FOR A NEW GENERATION

Within a few weeks of the publication of "One Great Christian Essential: 'Be Filled with the Spirit,'" Nazi Germany attacked Poland beginning World War II in Europe. More than two years would elapse before the United States would be drawn into the war following the Japanese attack on Pearl Harbor in December 1941. In those darkening years Flower continued traveling to District Councils, preaching at ordination services and teaching Bible lessons. Four of his children were now active in ministry; Rossie was a student at CBI; only David was still in high school. Obviously, the delay of the Lord's coming was leading to the rise of a new generation of Pentecostals who were going to face a rapidly changing world. What did these young men and women and their pastors and leaders need to know? The short answer was Scripture and history. The question of history had captured Flower's attention years earlier and would become even more central to his thinking. We will explore this area of his thought in chapter 8.

From his conversion, J. Roswell had been deeply committed to the authority of Scripture. The biblical teaching on the baptism in the Holy Spirit, the Trinity, and on prophecy were central to his study and preaching, as were other doctrines identified in the Statement of Fundamental Truths. Hermeneutical issues were also important; his 1936 article "In the House of the Interpreter" in the *Pentecostal Evangel* argued for the central role of the Pauline Epistles (including Hebrews) for interpreting the Old Testament. Flower pressed a key point: readers should not build doctrinal arguments from OT Scriptures without subjecting them to the light of the apostolic epistles. The New Testament interprets the Old, not the other way around. Flower emphasized the role of the Holy Spirit as the divine interpreter of the Bible as he also had inspired and guided revelation. Hermeneutics was not simply a rational or imaginative linking of the texts of Scripture; it was a careful attempt to identify the spiritual meaning intended by the Holy Spirit. Scripture was to guide Christian living and service as well as doctrine. Understanding the Word rightly was crucial for the church.

As a district superintendent and as the General Secretary, Flower taught the use of the Bible for guidance in Christian service, noting the role of the Holy Spirit in the process. The most important aspect of ministerial and missionary commitment was a clear knowledge of the "call of God," the title of his sermon at the Lake Geneva Camp in Minnesota in the summer of 1938, not long before leaving for Africa. First Corinthians 1 and Romans 1:1–6 served as the texts to unfold a biblical paradigm for grasping and obeying the call of God on one's life for pastoral and missionary work. The outbreak of World War II gave urgency to men and women being clear about God's calling, especially, those who were younger, the new generation.

Flower deepened his message relating the Bible to service in "There Was a Man." The biblical narrative from Abraham forward through the New Testament revealed that when God wanted to accomplish some specific work among human beings, he more often than not chose an individual through whom to work. Flower made explicit in the published version of the message that the generic "man" in the scripture text (John 1:6) meant both men and women. This biblical pattern should not be confined to the past. God revealed a pattern he continued to follow. He still called those whom he chose. Being assured of one's call, a man or a woman could also be sure that God intended to accomplish some task through them. Such knowledge was fundamental in the face of war, persecution, social upheaval, natural disasters, famines, plagues, and more, if one was to be steadfast in the will of God. He pointed to D. L. Moody in America and to an unnamed European missionary in Uganda (he learned the story while there) who persevered through the loss of all his colleagues to plant the gospel in eastern Africa. A written version of "There Was a Man" published in the *C. A. Herald* was addressed to the youth of the next generation. Its message was powerful: individual readers of the article might be chosen and called according to the biblical pattern. As a hermeneutical insight, J. Roswell believed that one should read the Bible not simply for the principles in the Wisdom literature or the doctrines in the Epistles, but also for the theology and guidance of the narrative patterns.

Six months to the day before the Japanese attack on Pearl Harbor, J. Roswell's Central Bible Institute Baccalaureate address, "Approved in Christ," was published in the *Pentecostal Evangel*. The outcome of the war in Europe looked increasingly dark for the Allied Powers in mid-1941. Missionary work in Europe, Africa, and the Middle East was more and more hindered, travel often difficult, and supplies of all kinds reduced. The situation in the Pacific also was increasingly dangerous as Japan extended its Imperial control in China, Southeast Asia, and over some of the Pacific islands. It was not an auspicious time to graduate from Bible school with a desire to become a missionary. Flower did not focus on this world tempest; instead, he addressed the most important dimension of the graduates' lives, "Approved in Christ" (Rom 16:10). It is not enough, he told the graduates, to be intellectually able to "rightly divide the word of truth," though that was necessary. After all, the goal of education was to give persons some basic knowledge. More important, education was to teach them how to learn, and to acquaint the students with the discipline necessary for learning. One's education was never finished; he or she would not go far in life without developing a deeper practical life of fellowship with God and a more extensive comprehension of a wide range of knowledge both divine and secular. The goal of being approved in Christ was to have a life that was "naturally spiritual, and spiritually natural all the time." He told his audience, "What we have of the gospel written down deep in our hearts is the only thing that counts after all."

CONCLUSION

"Back to Calvary," Flower's 1935 General Council sermon, was an appeal to the first generation of Pentecostals to move forward by reclaiming a central doctrine and experience of early Pentecostalism. The baptism in the Holy Spirit was an enduement of power for service, not sanctification. Pentecost followed the cross and would not exist without the latter. The sermon also marked Flower's growing awareness that a new generation was coming of age and its members needed to know the doctrines and experiences of the early days so that they might appropriate them for themselves. Scripture was the crucial heart of how people knew the meaning of the cross and Spirit-baptism and provided the guidance needed to lay hold of them by faith. Furthermore, as he focused on Christian service in the years before the War, he saw with increasing clarity the need for the new generation to understand the history of the Pentecostal movement as the outflow of the providences of God.

Return to National Office

US entry into World War II forced Flower to refocus his attention on other matters for several years. We turn to those in the next chapter.

7

Avoiding Sectarianism

> I feel that as long as I am in this fellowship, I have a duty for the upholding of the principles of that original declaration of constitution. I know the spirit that drew us together in the beginning, . . . God help us to keep the spirit of sectarianism out of our hearts.
>
> —J. Roswell Flower, "The Snare of Sectarianism"

J. Roswell Flower came to see more and more the value of the original principles of the General Council (unity, voluntary cooperation, fellowship) as the years passed. He was also aware of the threats to them as the Assemblies of God family grew larger in the United States and its missionary force expanded in the world. What he dreaded was the possibility that these principles would cease to be the working ones of the General Council and in their place would be an organization ruled from the top down for its own goals and the interest of its leaders. This would be a form of unity, a coerced one—one that would exclude the freedom and sovereignty of the local assemblies so prized by the founders and first-generation leaders.

Avoiding Sectarianism

UNITY, COOPERATION, FELLOWSHIP

Between the two world wars, European Pentecostals had begun to explore the possibility of a greater cooperation among the various national bodies. Obviously, the outbreak of a second war delayed further discussions. Flower was aware of these discussions and in the postwar 1940s and 50s would add a North American voice to them. The disruptions to the churches and missions caused by the war (even before US entry) seemed to have prodded him to examine the two kinds of unity he saw in Scripture and in history. In the October 18, 1941 issue of the *Pentecostal Evangel*, he published "Cooperation and Fellowship in the Present World Crisis." The Genesis account of the Tower of Babel and the Nazi dictatorship in Germany revealed the power of a unity set in opposition to God, a unity to do evil. God said with reference to the Babel conspiracy, "Behold, the people is one, and they have all one language; and this they begin to do: and now nothing will be restrained from them, which they have imagined to do" (Gen 11:6). The Nazis were demonstrating for evil on the battlefields and in their nation and occupied lands a historical instance of that statement. However, J. Roswell argued that unity among believers (Psalm 133) to do the will of God could accomplish much for the kingdom of God and for good in the world. Three decades earlier, Flower had used Genesis 11:6 to emphasize the power of unity for evangelism.

The Assemblies of God itself was another historical instance of the principle that unity increases the power to accomplish goals. He drew on his first-hand knowledge of Lake Victoria as a metaphor. The lake was formed by many rivers and streams flowing into it from the south, east, and west, creating a large, placid body of water. On the north, the waters spilled down over the falls becoming the origin of the Nile River, which flowed northward for thousands of miles to the Mediterranean Sea, creating a ribbon of life through the vast desert. Just so, the General Council had been created by the flowing together of many small Pentecostal streams into the body of the Assemblies of God in 1914, and, through the twenty-seven years since, had been flowing throughout the world giving life to hundreds of thousands of lost and dying men, women, and children. Flower demonstrated that this unity was nearly lost within two years of the founding. However, "Unity in Spirit" was preserved in the midst of the New Issue crisis at the 1915 General Council when the delegates agreed to spend a year carefully studying the Bible's teachings on the nature of the Godhead before declaring what was scriptural and what unscriptural in the debate. "Unity of belief" was preserved at the 1916 Council by the majority acceptance of the "Statement of Fundamental Truths" (SFT) as a biblically accurate summary of the essential doctrines Pentecostals should hold and teach in common. The preservation of this twofold unity of Spirit and faith secured the continuous flowing of the "full-gospel." Cooperation and fellowship were carried on in both defined experience and sound teaching. J. Roswell reminded his readers that this authority to declare what was scriptural and unscriptural in doctrine and practice was specifically given to the General Council (not simply executives) in the "Preamble and Resolution on Constitution" approved at Hot Springs in April 1914. The ultimate goal of the three principles was Spirit-empowered evangelism at home and abroad to reap the harvest before Jesus returned.

Less than two months after the publication of Flower's article, the United States was drawn into the war as a result of the attack on Pearl Harbor by an Axis nation. In Europe the war had been going on for more than two years. The multitude of prophecies and prophetic speculations that had accompanied the outbreak of World War I a quarter century earlier was muted with the new war. J. Roswell's son, Rossie, a student at Central Bible Institute, asked his father about prophecy and the European conflict. He responded to Rossie in a letter. Time had proven the spoiler of nearly all "prophecies" generated by the first war; Christ had not returned in 1914, 1917, or even 1933. Furthermore, even J. Roswell's own attempts to interpret biblical prophecies in relation to current events proved fallacious. Flower told his son the only certain thing he believed was the soon-coming of Christ. All other attempts to identify the exact relationship between biblical texts and things like the ten-kingdom confederation of the antichrist, the identity of the antichrist himself, and so forth, were tenuous at best and probably futile. He no longer was indulging in such speculations.

US entrance into the war created significant difficulties in maintaining the principles of unity, voluntary cooperation, and fellowship at both the national and international levels. National participation in the war led Flower to address the question of how to pray for America as a combatant nation. Many were, of course, proclaiming the righteousness and innocence of the nation over against the evil of the Axis powers: Germany, Italy, Japan, and their allies. Flower had for several years lamented the growing worldliness and decline of public morality in the United States of America. To believe the nation to be righteous before God would lead to the wrong kind of prayers. The nation's real condition before God was that of a people that had long been forgetting God. We "are now getting our just desserts," he asserted in the May 9, 1942 *Pentecostal Evangel*. The prayer appropriate to the nation's true status was Daniel 9, the prayer of a penitent prophet among a sinful people. We were experiencing God's judgment, not suffering for righteousness sake. Christian citizens must confess their sins and those of the nation while praying for forgiveness and God's gracious intervention to save our nation. Unity was strained over the questions surrounding "patriotism."

At the same time, many Pentecostal male believers were faced with the problem of participation in the war effort at some level. Ministers and ministerial students (all of the Flower sons) were exempt but their numbers were small compared to the total numbers in the Fellowship. The General Council of the Assemblies of God had declared itself a pacifist communion during World War I and continued to hold that stance. However, individuals were free to believe and behave as their conscience directed them. This was not unusual; a large number of American churches took similar positions during the Great War. Yet, the period between the wars had witnessed a sea change on the question of war that directly influenced AG members and adherents. Fewer of them now opposed war and hence most men, who were called up for active duty, or volunteered, were not opposed to serving as combatants. Flower summarized their attitude as that of an executioner. The person acts on behalf of the state carrying out the legitimate use of governmental power to "bear the sword." No personal guilt is involved because the killing is not done for personal revenge or out of hatred. A soldier acts in the same capacity. This widespread attitude did make it difficult for those who either were opposed to participating in any way whatsoever in the war effort or were opposed to participating as combatants. Some of these latter served as clerks, dental or medical technicians, etc., even in combat zones without bearing arms. For all these objectors at whatever level, as General Secretary, J. Roswell wrote letters to draft (Selective Service) boards around the country affirming the official pacifist position to support the appeal of an individual draftee or volunteer to be granted conscientious-objector status.

Despite the relatively low level of use made of the conscientious-objector status provision, Flower argued that the official position of the AG ought to be maintained; it helped protect that most crucial of all freedoms, the freedom of religion, the freedom of individual conscience both to decide about and to live out religious principles. In all of his various writings, he did not unequivocally state his own position. In one article he noted the sharp distinction between the spirit of Christ (as an ethos) and the war spirit. They were antithetical. After the war, when the American government passed the Universal Military Training and Service Act (1951), Flower published his disapproval of it. The law he believed militarized the nation even in peacetime, leading to a psychology of war in place of peace.

Flower had long applied the GC principles to personal relations with non-Pentecostal Christians, especially fundamentalists and evangelicals. In the 1920s he cooperated with the crusades of Bob Jones Sr., even though Jones called tongues speaking demonic. J. Roswell reached out to him and established a relationship with Jones that eventually resulted in Jones granting him at Bob Jones College (University) an honorary Doctor of Laws degree several years later (1946). Further, Flower had a close fellowship with

Avoiding Sectarianism

David Kins, the African Methodist Episcopal Church pastor in Scranton, Pennsylvania, and with the Moravian Brethren Bishop in Lititz, Pennsylvania. The conditions that developed in America during the war called for an even more extended application of the General Council principles. The need for churches to unite around common problems regarding their public activities and proclamation was evident. Roman Catholics had their national organization to represent them before government; mainline Protestants had the Federal Council of Churches of Christ in America. Fundamentalists, Evangelicals, and Pentecostals, however, had no shared national body to represent them even though they faced common problems. Flower was attracted to a proposal by some evangelical leaders to found the National Association of Evangelicals (NAE); potentially, Pentecostals might belong.

A key reason besides evangelism he espoused the GC principles was to counteract sectarianism, which he called a snare in a *Pentecostal Evangel* article. Sectarianism was a hindrance to unity, cooperation, and fellowship. Flower saw it working in three ways in America. His greatest fear was its getting a foothold in the General Council, undermining the Council principles and subverting the sovereignty of local assemblies by giving too much power to the leadership. He also saw how sectarianism blocked the cooperative, united efforts of "evangelical Christians" in the public square at a time when such action was desperately needed. Third, in a rare political statement, especially in wartime, he expressed what he thought would be the effects of a sort of secular sectarianism developing in America. The presidential use of executive orders and the establishing of departments exempt from judicial review, excluding citizen participation via the legislative branch of government, were altering the United States irrevocably. Postwar America would be a very different place than it was before 1941. Power would flow from the top down, whether in nation or church, a Babel-like organization would result; hence, Flower's heart-cry for God to keep sectarianism out of the hearts of men and women in the Fellowship.

J. Roswell Flower

On the basis of the principles he had held for thirty years, J. Roswell promoted Assemblies of God participation in the NAE. He attended the constitutional convention of the association in the spring of 1943, becoming one of the early leaders. He argued for General Council approval of the Fellowship's long term NAE membership at the Council meeting that August. After the war, he published writings supporting the Assemblies' continuing membership in the Association for three reasons: first, the AG still needed to participate in a united voice on common "moral and religious questions" in America; second, the Fellowship could continue to use common Sunday school materials that did not limit its distinctive doctrine and teaching on the baptism in the Holy Spirit; and third, the profound compassion needs of postwar Europe as well as other portions of the world called for united effort. NAE collection and administering of aid through the churches antedated the Marshall Plan by at least two years. On the ground in Europe and elsewhere, local Pentecostal churches would receive and distribute the aid. This would, he argued, not only bless people materially, give them a cup of cold water, but would also open the door for proclaiming the gospel. Compassion ministry and verbal witness were to go hand in hand.

After the war, Flower participated in the formation of two other organizations that were extensions of the General Council principles, the Pentecostal Fellowship of North America and the World Pentecostal Fellowship. He believed that the unity expressed in these two organizations along with the NAE indicated that the coming of Jesus was very near. Each group promoted in its own way the advancement of the kingdom of God and the evangelization of the world. Wars and rumors of wars (rife during the Cold War years) were negative signs of the Lord's return; but the spread of the gospel to the whole world was to lead directly to the rapture of believers.

LOSS AND HOPE

The Flowers had experienced two notable healings of their children: Joseph had smallpox during their first residence in Springfield in the early 1920s. J. Roswell had to sleep on a cot in his office for the duration of the illness because the house was quarantined. In the late 1920s in Scranton, David had been healed of a deadly bronchial infection. When in mid-November of 1941, shortly before Pearl Harbor, God chose not to heal their next-to-youngest child, Roswell Stanley, age twenty-one, they did not complain. Confident that he was in the presence of the God he loved and was serving, they wept and rejoiced simultaneously. Rossie was one semester away from graduation at Central Bible Institute (CBI). Afflicted with a weak heart, he died from overexertion changing a flat tire on his car on a cold, rainy night returning from a meeting at a CBI outstation. Their sorrow and hope presaged that of many American parents over the next four years. Thousands of young men and women who might have become pastors, teachers, deacons, and church leaders were lost; some died, some lost their faith, some simply became indifferent to things of God. On the other hand, some returned with a new fire in their souls to serve God. With the new generation of students who were too young to serve in the military, these returning troops needed Bible college education. Into this generation J. Roswell invested his best thought and called his own generation in North America and Europe to give their best to those who were preparing to take up the task of making and training disciples around the world. Two addresses he gave will help illustrate this commitment.

At age sixty-four in 1952 he stood before the Welsh Presbytery in Cardiff, Wales. "I believe," he told them, "God has definitely brought the Pentecostal movement into existence for a certain ministry to this generation." It was a generation faced at every turn with materialism, agnosticism, and secular humanism. To lose "this generation" would be to lose the movement. How was the new generation to know Pentecost? It must be passed on by Flower and the presbyters' generation in purity of life and by living a gospel of power. They must live what they expected their sons and daughters to receive and practice.

The power, of course, came via the baptism in the Holy Spirit; purity of life came through embracing the cross. Flower had preached it at the 1935 General Council and repeated it many times over the intervening years, there can be no Pentecost without Calvary. Near the end of his long service as General Secretary he offered another meditation on the cross. His sermon "The Cross in Christian Service" was the commencement address to Central Bible College (formerly CBI) graduates in 1959. The sermon was subsequently published in the *Pentecostal Evangel*. The work of the cross in Christian service involved the daily discipline of taking up one's cross and following Christ. Flower developed three implications: first, Bible college was only the beginning. One has only learned how to learn; the serious work commences with graduation. Education was never finished. The secular dimensions were always expanding, there was always more to know. Religiously, the cross called one to a disciplined learning of biblical and theological matters. Furthermore, one's education prior to Bible school was not to be discounted; it was to be yielded to God through the cross to be used redemptively as one served. Most important, if secular education and religious education were ongoing, even more so was spiritual education. J. Roswell emphasized knowing the "providences of God" in one's life. This required drawing near to God that he might teach a person the ways his hand guided one up to that point. Grasping God's ways with oneself enhanced his or her knowledge of God and stimulated fellowship with the living God. Submitting daily to the work of the cross in one's life maximized the use the Holy Spirit made of his or her education in serving Christ and others. Such submission was itself a spiritual education as one came to know God more fully and intimately.

CONCLUSION

Over time, Flower came to believe that the principles embodied in the General Council—unity, voluntary cooperation, and fellowship—were providentially given and established. They were simple enough to guide local assemblies and capacious enough to guide a world fellowship. So too the practical outworking of the baptism in the Holy Spirit and the doctrine of the cross were central to individuals and the entire Pentecostal movement. As the years passed without the return of Christ, Flower realized the necessity of clearly and carefully transmitting the faith to the next generation. How could that best be done? What did the upcoming generation need to know, experience, and practice?

8

Historian and Statesman

> Doctrinal positions are not usually arrived at as the result of independent study and research. They are handed down to us from our forefathers and are largely the result of environment.
>
> —J. ROSWELL FLOWER, *CHURCH ORIENTATION*

IN APRIL 1951, FLOWER was invited to be a chapel speaker at Drury College (University) in Springfield, Missouri. The occasion followed some international trips but was before his more extensive world travels from 1952 through the end of the decade. He noted the resurgent general interest in religion in postwar America and remarked on the significant differences between the historical, social, cultural, and spiritual impact of Christianity and that of Marxism, rationalism, and non-biblical religions. Reflecting on his travels to date in Europe, the Middle East, and Africa in the late 1930s and 40s, he said two things stood out to him. First, he came to believe that human beings are instinctively religious. Second, he observed that the "religion of Jesus Christ" had a greater impact for good than all other religions and philosophies. Why? The answer Flower gave was embedded in the text he chose for the Drury talk,

Psalm 115:2–8, especially verse 8: "They that make them [idols] are like unto them; so is everyone that trusteth in them." A people's "god(s)" essentially determined the character of their culture and civilization.

J. Roswell had a deep, abiding love for America; he loved its democracy, especially religious liberty, and that, he argued, was rooted in Christianity. For several years he and Alice had observed the increasing secularization of American public education. When their oldest child, Joseph, was a high school student in Scranton, Pennsylvania, in the late 1920s, they were concerned about the teaching of science from a naturalistic point of view. Naturalistic rationalism had spread into much of the rest of the curriculum as well through the 1930s and 40s. Flower increasingly called for Assemblies of God congregations to begin Christian schools and for members and adherents of the assemblies to send their children to Christian schools. In the 1950s he avidly supported the opening of Evangel College and urged parents whose children were not called into full-time ministry to send them to Evangel. If they were called into full-time ministry, they should attend one of the Bible colleges operated by the General Council. His deep concern was that the increase of naturalistic rationalism in American colleges and universities—also, reflected in modernism's impact on liberal religious schools—would corrupt the minds of students, turning them away from Christian faith. The consequences would be the loss of souls and a decline in the quality of American public life and education. When the US Supreme Court ruled in *McCollum v. Board of Education* (1948) that the Champaign, Illinois school district could not facilitate religious instruction for those who wanted it, Flower argued that religious freedoms in public schools would be restricted. In short, if America's god were scientific, naturalistic rationalism, the nation would become deaf to God, blind to moral truths, and dumb to justice and righteousness.

J. Roswell Flower

PENTECOSTAL HISTORIAN

Far more important to Flower than the quality of American public life was his concern for the spiritual life of the Assemblies of God. He had since 1925 been periodically looking back over the life of the Fellowship to evaluate its progress. He wrote and spoke about the history of the Pentecostal movement and the AG Fellowship for more than forty years. His backward gaze was not antiquarianism. He believed revival movements were birthed and matured over time. Studying the past of a movement helped one understand whether or not it was developing and maturing or declining, atrophying. Understanding where the Fellowship was in the growth process aided national and district officials, ministers, missionaries, and others in praying for the leading of the Holy Spirit and encouraged them to cooperate with him in obedience to the Lordship of Christ. The twofold goal was evangelism and discipleship, winning souls and preparing the church as the bride of Christ for his return. Studying the past was not, then, a call to return to the "good old days"; it was an appeal for the new generations to appropriate for themselves the blessings God stood ready to pour out on them as he had on their parents. Though many religion scholars, then (and now), believed revival movements naturally peaked and declined, Flower did not agree that decline was inevitable. Continued vibrancy was possible as members and adherents sought the Holy Spirit to continue his work in their lives, keeping them "filled with the Holy Spirit." After all, the Pentecostal movement was not a "natural" phenomenon. (In a sense, Flower anticipated some of the subsequent scholarly writing about Pentecostalism and rejected it.)

There were several insights Flower brought to or gleaned from the scrutiny of the past: first, movements pass through phases. In 1925 he thought the AG had moved through two phases and was at a critical third one that required specific decisions on the part of first-generation leaders and members. The early experiences and doctrinal disputes were behind the Fellowship. It faced the question of its uniqueness, its difference. Some religious groups failed because they were unwilling to be different. If Pentecostals were unwilling to bear the cross of rejection by fundamentalists, some evangelicals, and liberals because of Spirit-baptism evidenced by speaking in tongues, they would wither up and become one more sect or denomination. A second insight had come to Flower with the passage of time. Twenty years later at the closing of World War II (1945), Christ had not returned as the first generation had expected. A new generation was on the scene; what did the members of that new generation need to know about the past in order to maintain the revival flow of the movement? Speaking to the Youth Conference (1945) attendees in Springfield, Missouri, Flower took six lectures to detail "Our Pentecostal Heritage" for them. Half a century had passed since the sporadic outpourings of the Holy Spirit in various places, forty-five years since the outpouring in Topeka, thirty-nine since Azusa began, and thirty-one since the Hot Springs general council. In order to tell the teenagers sitting before him what they needed to know, Flower had to rethink the periodization of the movement.

Without specifying time markers, he argued that the first phase of the Fellowship was characterized by a deep hunger for God, the presence of miracles, and simplicity of doctrine. However, hunger waned, miracles declined, and doctrine necessarily became complicated in order to deal with conflicts over sanctification, the rise of the New Issue, and the formation of a doctrinal standard, the "Statement of Fundamental Truths." Did these things indicate decline in the revival? Not necessarily, Flower thought. After all, with the presence of the Statement of Fundamental Truths, even though miracles declined, evangelism burst forth with great vigor, marking a second phase of the Fellowship's maturation. Importantly, this evangelistic phase did not deny the distinctive of the Assemblies of God, the baptism in the Holy Spirit. In fact, quite the contrary was true: bold evangelism relied on the empowering of the Holy Spirit. Evangelistic campaigns added to the numbers of assemblies and members; also, with the passage of time, children and grandchildren of first-generation members were now on the verge of taking their place in the adult fellowship. The AG, he argued, was at a third phase that overlapped with the second. The phase the new generation before him faced involved a revival in education. They needed not only the experience of the baptism; they needed to know the history of the movement to understand how it came to have its emphases, doctrines, practices, and GC principles. This was not a matter of having knowledge of a past that determined the future. Instead, Flower believed that a careful grasp of the relevant aspects of the past encouraged the saints' intelligent cooperation with the Holy Spirit to continue the flow of the Pentecostal river. It was this history he was teaching them in the lectures they were hearing, he believed. This re-periodizing of the Pentecostal Movement was the second crucial insight Flower had into its history.

A third major insight must have come to Flower during the time of the youth lectures or shortly thereafter. In a year or two after the conference, these students would graduate high school. Some would become students at Central Bible Institute (College) or another GC school. Others, not called in to ministry, would attend non-AG Christian colleges; some would go to state-sponsored institutions. Already Flower had realized the need for Christian schools. What was needed for the graduating high school students not called into full-time ministry was a Pentecostal liberal arts college. The revival of education meant that the Fellowship needed to mature with regard to higher education. His support for the building of Evangel College was severely criticized by some who believed liberal arts education would result in corrupting the youth of the movement.

Flower had himself been teaching in Bible schools and summer Bible camps since the teen years of the twentieth century. He taught at T. K. Leonard's school in Findlay, Ohio in 1914 and at Central Bible Institute in Springfield, Missouri when it first opened in the early 1920s. When he moved to the Eastern District, he taught at Bethel Bible Training School in Newark, New Jersey and later at the Maranatha Park Summer Bible School in the 1930s. Returning to Springfield as general secretary, he had begun teaching at CBI again. For several years he regularly taught a course on Pentecostal/Assemblies of God history for which he wrote a manual titled *Church Orientation* (1950). His continuous rehearsing of the story led him to a fourth major insight, a revisionist one on AG history. The strong restorationist position, premised on the notion that the Pentecostal Early Rain (speaking in tongues and miraculous gifts) stopped in about the third or fourth century and suddenly began falling again as the Latter Rain at Topeka and Azusa Street at the beginning of the twentieth century, did not match the historical evidence. No, he argued, church history revealed that charismatic manifestations had continued right on through the medieval period, the Reformation age, and the eighteenth and nineteenth centuries. Furthermore, most of the doctrines and practices of the Assemblies of God had antecedents in the nineteenth century and very early-twentieth-century evangelical, holiness, and healing movements. God had been preparing for the Latter Rain outpouring for several decades; that is the way he works in human history, Flower declared. The AG had a distinct testimony, but it was not unique. It was wonderfully a continuation of the story of redemption that was nearing its consummation. Pentecostal students needed to see where they and their Fellowship fit into the large story of God's salvation purposes in human history so that they might seek to fulfill God's purposes for the movement by receiving the baptism in the Holy Spirit, by seeking to "be filled with the Holy Spirit" always, and by engaging in the greatest movement for evangelism the world had seen.

After the end of World War II and the beginning of recovery in Europe and elsewhere, European Pentecostals resumed efforts to have a World Pentecostal Conference. In 1954, J. Roswell was in England as a member of the planning committee for the triennial conference to convene in Stockholm, Sweden in 1955, at which he was to speak. Preparing for his address gave him opportunity to extend his understanding of the Pentecostal Movement. He had often retold the story to American audiences of the "birth of the Pentecostal Movement." How did Europeans, Africans, and Asians fit into the story? The answer to that question was a fifth insight Flower had into the history of the twentieth-century Pentecostal

Movement—largely speaking, it was one movement from a single source. Exactly when the light dawned on him is not clear. Alice wrote to her mother-in-law, Bethia Flower (the only remaining parent they had), from aboard the ship taking them to Europe that "Roswell" was working on his address in transit. Maybe the flash was mid-Atlantic.

First, he needed to establish the question of the "genesis." Granting that the origin of the Church of God and the outpouring at Mukti Mission in India might not fit smoothly into his scheme and granting that there were outpourings of the Holy Spirit accompanied with tongues-speech in the nineteenth century, nonetheless, he argued, the movement had its defining moment in Topeka, Kansas on January 1, 1901, when Agnes N. Ozman spoke in tongues. She and her fellow students had determined that the biblical sign of (the initial physical evidence of) Spirit-baptism was tongues-speech. Having made that decision, they were tarrying expectantly for God to send the promise of the Holy Spirit with the sign.[*] When she, then others, spoke in tongues, they interpreted that as *the* sign. It was that event with that interpretation that was the "birth," the "genesis," of the worldwide movement. What happened in Topeka was carried to Houston and on to Los Angeles from where it spanned the globe. Nearly every person in that auditorium in Stockholm traced the roots of his or her church back to Azusa Street. However, there would have been no Azusa without Topeka—there was the birth. J. Roswell had linked the American story to the Jerusalem story already. In Stockholm, he presented a narrative that incorporated most of the various Pentecostal groups represented at the conference into a shared story of origins. He interpreted the story in such a way as to establish a world community that transcended nationalities and denominations—a World Pentecostal Conference rooted in unity, voluntary cooperation, and fellowship.

---

[*] Some contemporary historians hold that the actual order of these events was the reverse.

Historian and Statesman

PENTECOSTAL STATESMAN

Flower's address at the World Pentecostal Conference in Stockholm was an act of statesmanship as well as the meditation of a historical thinker. In the midst of a multitude of things that divided the delegates—nationality, doctrines, polity, and more—he created a community on the bases of common historical origins, shared experience, and shared goals. The response to his speech was immediate. Many called for it to be printed; it was, the next day. All those copies were quickly snatched up and another printing was necessary to meet the demand. It was subsequently published both in *The Pentecostal Testimony* and the *Pentecostal Evangel*.

In the early 1940s, J. Roswell had grasped the importance of joining with evangelicals in forming the National Association of Evangelicals (NAE). He noted that they all faced common problems and would benefit from a voluntary association that left each denomination the freedom to hold its distinctive testimony. They fellowshipped around a shared acceptance of biblical authority, a commitment to the new birth through faith in Christ, a common doctrinal core, and a strong commitment to evangelism and missions. Flower used the General Council of the Assemblies of God Minister's Letter as a platform to explain the value of belonging to the NAE and encouraging AG minsters to join the association. At one point, the Assemblies made up the largest denominational block of attendees at the national meetings. Similarly, he was an active participant and officer in the Pentecostal Fellowship of North America formed a few years after the NAE. His vision of the body of Christ, his ability to see the relationship of the Assemblies of God as a fellowship to other faith communities, and his grasp of how to establish relationships that promoted the kingdom of God in the nation and world were the marks of a statesman.

Flower knew that Christians are in the world but not of it. Being in the world, however, meant that the saints shared many common dimensions of life with their fellow citizens and human beings. When the General Council of the Assemblies of God moved to Springfield, Missouri in 1918, he seemed to have a sense of the rightness of establishing ties of friendship between headquarters and the community. He personally made the acquaintance of merchants, professionals, and bankers along Commercial Street. In Scranton, Pennsylvania, he joined the local ministerial association and had opportunity to pray with and for ministers of mainstream Protestant churches; through these contacts he even counselled political leaders. The experience was not lost on him. As a district superintendent and the general secretary, Flower urged Assemblies pastors to be a part of ministerial associations and spread their influence by intelligent sharing of their faith and understanding.

When the Flowers returned to Springfield in the mid-1930s, he began once more to participate in the life of the city. He, Alice, and Adele all loved the local symphony concerts and purchased season tickets. Flower attended the weekly meetings of the Commercial Club and became a speaker for Kiwanis and Rotary Clubs. The Community Chest, Chamber of Commerce, Boy Scouts (which also invited him to be one of four Protestant chaplains at one National Jamboree), and the Salvation Army all invited him to serve on their Boards. The Sertoma Club honored him with an award for service to humanity. The YMCA honored him for twelve years of service as a member of their World Service committee. Possibly the crowning civic achievement was an eight-year period of service as a Springfield City Councilman between 1953 and 1961. It was, he believed, a way of serving both God and his fellow citizens.

A statesman must have a substantial knowledge of relevant history and the wisdom and insight to see its applicability to the present situation. He also needs to be able to discern "where" in history the present situation is occurring and determine a wise course of action for the future. Flower found a key to this kind of insight in his concept of the providence of God. It informed both his interpretation of the Pentecostal movement and his understanding of the life of a Pentecostal saint, his own included. Of the movement at large, he held that each step in the maturation of the revival brought the church nearer the fulfillment of God's purpose for the GC. Unity, voluntary cooperation, and fellowship enhanced the Spirit-empowered church's efforts to evangelize the world and disciple the next generation, hastening the coming of the Lord. Cooperation between Pentecostals and Evangelicals and Fundamentalists forwarded their common task of world missions. Flower did not lose sight of the individual in this big picture. The cross was the heart of the shared theology of these groups. The cross was the necessary experience of the individual believer.

In 1959, J. Roswell delivered the commencement address at CBC, "The Cross in Christian Service," later published in the *Pentecostal Evangel*. He connected the providence of God and the cross in the life of the servant of God. The initial surrender of a sinner to the cleansing of the cross (as Christ's crucifixion for him or her) brought one into the family of God. Fruitful service for Christ could only follow surrendering to the cross (as crucifixion of one's self-will), yielding to the Lordship of Christ and the guidance of the Holy Spirit in every area of one's life and ministry. Flower drew on the life of Saul/Paul to illustrate how God's providences (with special attention to training and education) and the cross work together in one's life. Saul's life and education fit him well to be the Pharisee he was; how did it fit into the life of "Paul." When he yielded to the cross, he discovered years later how that education and experience equipped him to stand before the Sanhedrin and Roman officials and judges. Just so, Flower told his audience, especially the graduates, they should look for God's providences in their lives, including all previous education and training. Do not discount it, he argued, God ordered it and can use it for his glory in your life when it is surrendered to the cross.

In an analogous way, the providences of God led to the outpouring of the Holy Spirit in the twentieth century and also, within that large movement, to the establishing of the Assemblies of God. If the members (leaders and others) of the General Council turned away from experiencing and declaring the cross and the baptism in the Holy Spirit, they would fail to fulfill the purposes of God for the movement as would an individual fail personally who ceased to follow Christ.

J. Roswell Flower

CONCLUSION

Historians and statesmen contribute significantly to the self-understanding of people, as persons and especially as groups of one kind or another. J. Roswell Flower's mature thought about the identity and meaning of the General Council of the Assemblies of God had developed over the decades as he studied, taught, and wrote the story of the twentieth-century Pentecostal movement. Through his teaching, speaking, writing, and tireless service, he informed an international audience of Pentecostal, evangelical, and fundamentalist Christians about "Pentecost." He did this in ways that affirmed for Pentecostals the distinct niche they had in the body of Christ and emphasized the inestimable value of maintaining both the actual experience of the baptism in the Holy Spirit and their faithful witness to the biblical testimony in which it was anchored. He, furthermore, refused to reject or denigrate men and women and the churches they served who differed with him about Spirit-baptism but were true to the "fundamentals" of the faith. He was a founding father for Pentecostals with a generous spirit toward others.

Conclusion and Legacy

A YEAR AFTER J. Roswell Flower committed himself to follow Jesus Christ as Lord and Savior, he began a journal he called "My Diary: The Fads and Fancies of a 'Foolish Fellow.'" He kept the record for slightly over two years, between roughly age twenty and twenty-two. Reading the diary, one "observes" two things: the exciting growth of a heart in love with God and the awakening of a mind committed to learning so that he might be useful in the Lord's service. The "foolish fellow" who began the account grew into a faithful follower of Christ Jesus. The trajectory of Flower's life was set, heart and mind, in the service of the King.

When the nineteen-year-old Flower became a consecrated follower of Jesus Christ at a Pentecostal mission in Indianapolis in 1907, the movement was only seven years old. It had grown slowly until a year before Flower's conversion when it exploded, spreading flames of revival all across the nation and even the world from Los Angeles. (Many years later, Flower likened the Azusa Street revival to an atomic bomb that scattered radiation all over the world; the bomb had been built in Topeka.) He came to Christ in one of those places ignited by a flame from the Azusa Street Mission. He was chronologically a young man and spiritually a newborn. Born as he was in the first stage of the movement's history, he had six decades to grow with the movement. He did more than grow with the movement, however. Flower contributed directly to its growth. There was a reciprocal relationship between his maturation and that of the movement, especially in the form of the General Council of the Assemblies of God.

In the early stage of the movement irregular or monthly periodicals were issued by dozens of churches and individuals. It says something about both the movement and J. Roswell that he and Alice began publishing the first weekly magazine in 1913, which flourished into the early twenty-first century. By publishing news, testimonies, and doctrinal articles, Flower contributed to the spread of Pentecostalism and its unity. Unity among some of the multitude of Pentecostal groups coalesced around the formation of the General Council of the Assemblies of God. Flower was there in Hot Springs at the inaugural meeting and was elected general secretary. His growth as a leader and the development of what he presciently called an epoch-making meeting set the direction of the twenty-five year old for the rest of his life, more than fifty-six years. He served in national offices most of the next eleven years, bearing the weight of financial hardship, divisive doctrinal disputes, and making difficult and unpopular decisions to adjust to the growth of the Assemblies of God and the rapidly changing post-WWI world.

For a decade Flower served as local pastor and district official far from the Midwestern portion of the United States, learning firsthand the diversity of the Assemblies of God accompanying its growth. By 1935 when he was elected once again to the office of general secretary, the Fellowship needed the kind of leader he had grown to be. He understood deeply the principles of the General Council and knew practically how to implement them at multiple levels. He had experienced profoundly the power of the Holy Spirit and was irrevocably committed to the classical Pentecostal understanding of the baptism in the Holy Spirit.

J. Roswell was approaching fifty when he took the general secretary's position, an age at which many men begin slackening the pace of their lives and becoming resistant to change. Flower did neither. The fellowship had reached a level of maturity but needed to be interpreted and guided forward to further stages of growth. Flower's commitment to life-long learning of mind and

Conclusion and Legacy

spirit equipped him both to grasp the narrative of the movement and to suggest courses of action consistent with the past and the present. He advocated membership in the NAE; he participated both in its formation and in the forming of the Pentecostal Fellowship of North America and the World Pentecostal Fellowship. He was an avid supporter of a liberal arts college for the AG. He was able to provide new insight and to stimulate action consistent with the maturity level of the movement.

In his retirement years as his health failed, he was still looking forward. Flower saw no reason why the AG should decline; however, he knew full well that movements do change as generations come and go. When a new generation fails to appropriate the faith, beliefs, and practices that produced the growth of the first generation, it has no power to continue the vibrant life that preceded it. Decline is the consequence of the lack of power, of life flowing through the body—individually and collectively. If people recognize the decline and desire to change it, they may choose one of two courses of action: one is to move in a direction that does not forward the original life. The other is to seek to discover where the original impulse was lost, return to that point, and then move forward. The first course does not stop the decline of the institution's life; it masks the loss by feverish activity. Only the second, which involves repentance of sin and appropriating once again the benefits of the cross of Christ and the baptism of the Holy Spirit, permits a genuine renewal of the waning life and a continuation of the mature unfolding of the movement. (See Appendix D.)

When J. Roswell Flower departed this life in July 1970, four of the six children born to him and Alice survived and were all active in ministry. Roswell Stanley (Rossie) had died in 1941 in his last year of Bible school. Only he of the six was not ordained. George Ernest had passed away at age fifty from a brain tumor. A former superintendent of the Southern New England District, at the time of his illness and passing, he was a pastor in Penns Grove, New Jersey. Joseph Reynolds, the oldest of the children, lived to be ninety-seven. During his long life he was a pastor, the Superintendent of the New York District, and for many years General Secretary of the

J. Roswell Flower

AG. Alice Adele (m. Roy Dalton) served as a missionary in Latin America, and Spain before returning from the field to care for her mother. For several years she also worked in the foreign missions office at headquarters. Her incredible contribution to the history of the Assemblies of God missionary family has been recognized in the naming of the research and reading room of the Flower Pentecostal Heritage Center at the National Resources Center in her honor. She died at age ninety-one. Suzanne Grizelle (m. Albert Earle) went to her reward at age ninety-six as the manuscript for this book was being completed. She was a vibrant witness for Christ as a co-pastor with her husband and as a personal witness wherever she was. The one surviving child, the youngest of the six, David Warren is in his early-nineties. He helps teach the Sunday school class at Central Assembly of God his parents started in the 1930s and preaches one Sunday evening per month at the Maranatha Village Chapel, where he lives. He, too, served as a pastor, District Superintendent (Southern New England), and was at a critical period in the institution's history the Chairman of the Board of Evangel College (University).

This extraordinary family legacy prompted Donald Gee to write J. Roswell late in life and ask to what he attributed the remarkable faithfulness of his children. Flower responded that he wasn't sure but decided that two things were important: the daily family altar and his and Alice's efforts to live consistent lives, to live at home as they lived in the pulpit, the church, at Bible camp, etc., to live lives of true biblical holiness.

Apart from his influence on his children, Flower encouraged many pastors, missionaries, and earnest Christians around the world. Weakened by heart attacks, he still attended Central Assembly when he was able. One Sunday night in the later-1960s, he listened to a nervous young minister preach about the Holy Spirit. Very conscious of the presence of "Daddy" Flower in the audience, the man became even more nervous when he was told that the Fellowship patriarch had asked to see him following the service. Fearing the worst, he was greatly encouraged by the elder brother's affirmation, "that was the way we preached it in the early

Conclusion and Legacy

days." Dr. George O. Wood later served as General Superintendent of the Assemblies of God; he never forgot that word. Flower also deeply influenced the work of well-known Pentecostal historian, Dr. William W. Menzies. In the decade following Flower's retirement, Menzies interviewed him extensively for the official history, *Anointed to Serve: The Story of the Assemblies of God* (1970), which he dedicated to Flower. Shortly before his death, Menzies, who well-knew the foibles and follies of many Pentecostal leaders and was not given to careless adulation told this author "Flower was one of my heroes."

Appendix A
"Preamble and Resolution on Constitution"

WHEREAS, GOD, OUR HEAVENLY Father, sent His only begotten Son, the Lord Jesus Christ, into the world, Who purchased and redeemed fallen man with His own precious blood, and called out of the world and saved a people, of whom He built and established His church (Assembly of God—Mat. 16:18), upon the foundation of the Apostles and Prophets, Jesus Christ Himself being the Head and Chief Corner-stone (Eph. 2:20), and organized and baptized it with the Holy Spirit, with its government upon His shoulders (Isaiah 9:6–7), said: "The gates of hell shall not prevail against it" (Matt. 16:18), and

WHEREAS, He gave the Holy Inspired Scriptures, (both old and new covenants, Heb. 8:6–13) as the all-sufficient rule for faith and practice (2 Tim. 3:16), as follows: "All Scripture is given by inspiration of God, and is profitable for doctrine, for reproof, for correction, for instruction in righteousness: That the man of God may be perfect, thoroughly furnished unto all good works;" we therefore shall not add to nor take from it (Rev. 22:18); and

WHEREAS, He commanded that there should be no schism (division, sectarianism) in His body, the GENERAL ASSEMBLY (Church) of the first born, which are written in heaven, Heb. 12:23; and

WHEREAS, We recognize ourselves as members of said GENERAL ASSEMBLY OF GOD, (which is God's organism), and do not believe in identifying ourselves as, or establishing ourselves

Appendix A

into, a sect, that is a human organization that legislates or forms laws, and articles of faith and has unscriptural jurisdiction over its members and creates unscriptural lines of fellowship and disfellowship over its members and which separates itself from other members of the General Assembly (Church) of the first born, which is contrary to Christ's prayer in St. John 17, and Paul's teaching in Eph. 4:1–16, which we heartily endorse:

THEREFORE, BE IT RESOLVED, FIRST, That we recognize ourselves as a GENERAL COUNCIL of Pentecostal (Spirit Baptized) saints from local Churches of God in Christ, Assemblies of God, and various Apostolic Faith Missions and Churches, and Full Gospel Pentecostal Missions and Assemblies of like faith in the United States of America, Canada and Foreign Lands, whose purpose is neither to legislate laws of government, nor usurp authority over said various Assemblies of God, nor deprive them of their Scriptural and local rights and privileges, but to recognize Scriptural methods and order for worship, unity, fellowship, work and business for God, and disapprove of all unscriptural methods, doctrines and conduct, and approve of all Scriptural truth and conduct, endeavoring to keep the unity of the Spirit in the bonds of peace, until we all come into the unity of the faith, and of the knowledge of the Son of God, unto a perfect man, unto the measure of the stature of the fullness of Christ, and to walk accordingly, as recorded in Eph. 4:17–32, and to consider the five purposes announced in the Convention Call in the February, 1914, issue of "WORD AND WITNESS:"

RESOLVED, SECOND, That we recognize all the above said Assemblies of various names, and when speaking of them refer to them by the general Scriptural name "Assemblies of God:" and recommend that they all recognize themselves by the same name, that is, "Assembly of God" and adopt it as soon as practicable for the purpose of being more Scriptural and also legal in transacting business, owning property, and executing missionary work in home and foreign lands, and for general convenience, unity and fellowship.

"*Preamble and Resolution on Constitution*"

Minutes of the General Council of the Assemblies of God, April 2–12, 1914, pp. 4–5. Original spelling, punctuation, use of capitals, and word order has been retained throughout. Used by permission of the Flower Pentecostal Heritage Center.

Appendix B
"Back to Calvary"

THERE ARE TWO PASSAGES of Scripture that I wish to dwell upon in particular. The first is the 18th verse of the first chapter of Paul's first epistle to the Corinthians, "For the preaching of the cross is to them that perish foolishness; but unto us which are saved it is the power of God," and the 23rd and 24th of the same chapter, "But we preach Christ crucified, unto Jews a stumbling block, and unto the Greeks foolishness; but unto them which are called, both Jews and Greeks, Christ the power of God, and the wisdom of God. . . ."

The church at Corinth received the Word of God under the ministry of the Apostle Paul. He preached the Word in the power of the Spirit, and according to his own testimony determined to know nothing else among them save Jesus Christ and Him crucified. 1 Cor. 2:2. The Corinthians came under the influence of the gospel of Jesus Christ and the preaching of the Cross, and under that preaching they were saved and filled with the Holy Ghost just as were other believers in other cities.

It seems evident, however, that after Paul had departed for other fields of labor, much of Paul's influence waned. The keen edge of the message of the Cross was dulled, and the Corinthian church lapsed into carelessness and even into sin. That is the reason for the writing of the epistles to the Corinthian church. These epistles reveal that in almost every line of Christian conduct and of doctrine they had failed. They had failed in their choice of leaders, and divisions had resulted. They had let down in their

"Back to Calvary"

standards pertaining to the sexes, and sin had resulted. This sin had gone unrebuked. They had failed in their eating and drinking, and particularly in respect to meats that had been offered to idols. They had grown careless in their observance of the Communion of the Lord's table, and many had become sick and others had died. They failed in their conception of the true value and place for the manifestations of the Spirit in the assembly, and confusion had resulted. They even failed in their conception of the resurrection of the saints. In fact, the entire epistle to the Corinthians is devoted to correction and reproof.

Paul did not deny that they had received the Holy Spirit. He admitted that the church came behind in no gift and that they were enriched or made spiritually wealthy with all utterance and knowledge. And, yet, if this be true, how was such spiritual failure possible.

There can be only one answer. They had fallen away from the message of the Cross. There was a need of holding up before them once more the Cross of our Lord and Saviour Jesus Christ and of calling the church back to Calvary.

I have not forgotten the early days of our Pentecostal Movement. . . . Prayer groups were formed all over the country. . . .

Some of these prayer groups were characterized by the influence of the Cross of Christ by a remarkable degree. There was an earnest desire to separate from all the things of the world. There was no particular need to frown on worldliness in dress and deportment, for the very passion to please God was sufficient to bring separation from these things. Hours were spent in prayer. "Deeper yet, deeper yet" was the cry of all as they went down, down, down in the presence of God and wills were yielded to Him. . . .

I do not forget my own experience. I was saved in a Pentecostal meeting twenty-eight years ago. Many were the bitter tears that fell before that altar of prayer. The Lord dealt with my own heart in such a precious way. He dealt with my will, my desires, my plans and my purposes. He turned my life all around. I found that He had other plans than those of my choice. I had to lay everything at

Appendix B

His feet and embrace the Cross. I did so with tears, as I sought the face of the Lord. And then came my day of Pentecost. . . .

The Holy Spirit has been given as a direct result of Calvary. Sometimes I feel that we are apt to forget that fact. There would have been no Pentecost if there had not been Calvary. . . . So we found that the Holy Spirit would take us to Calvary, show us our need and the gracious provision for that need there. We would gaze upon Him, and tears of sorrow and of joy would flow. . . .

I believe that God sent this Pentecostal revival at a time when the world needed it the most. It is the only answer to the world's need for this present time. And yet, beloved, there is the possibility that the purposes of God in this revival will fail. . . .

I can tell you, there is no necessity for a declension if we will get back to Calvary, if we will come back to the foot of the Cross, if we will receive a fresh revelation of the blood of Jesus Christ. There is no necessity for a decline. We can go on in the power of the Spirit in that place to which the Lord has called us.

Calvary involves more than a presentation of the Cross of Christ to us, it has a practical application to your experience and to mine. There must be a deliberate choice on our part to take the way of the Cross. Paul made that choice deliberately. . . .

I feel this need in my life and in my own ministry. I feel sure that this is the need of our movement. Let us come back to the Cross of Christ and God will again manifest Himself to us in power.

Excerpted from: J. Roswell Flower, "Back to Calvary: Opening Message at the Sixteenth General Council of the Assemblies of God, by J. Roswell Flower, at Dallas, Texas, September 12, 1935." *Pentecostal Evangel* 1118 (October 5, 1935) 1, 10–11. Used by permission of the General Council of the Assemblies of God.

Appendix C
"One Great Christian Essential: 'Be Filled with the Spirit.'"

IT IS THE TRUTH of the Baptism in the Holy Spirit which has made us a distinct people. There are other great truths to which we adhere such as regeneration, sanctification, divine healing, and the imminent second coming of the Lord Jesus Christ, and these are all great truths, and essential to a full Gospel message, but none of them is responsible for making us a distinct people. These truths were held by many before the Assemblies of God were born. The one great truth which made us a distinct people is the Baptism in the Holy Spirit. If we were to minimize the truth of the Baptism in the Spirit or to step aside from its advocacy, we would be undermining our own testimony and our primary right for an existence as an organization. I believe this with all my heart. . . .

However, there are many things connected with the Pentecostal experience which we may have misunderstood. There is the danger of exalting an experience to a place of importance that is not given to it by the Word of God. . . .

. . . [T]here seems to be a feeling on the part of some that once we are baptized in the Holy Spirit, we are always baptized. . . . They fail to appreciate that the Baptism in the Holy Spirit is not a state at all. It is a sovereign act of God. That is, there was a time when they were baptized in the precious Holy Spirit—a definite time. . . .

Appendix C

If we once get this matter clear that the Baptism in the Holy Spirit is an act rather than a state, it will help us to understand the admonition found in the scripture before us [Eph. 5:13–20].... The Baptism in the Holy Spirit does introduce us into a realm where it is possible for us to be continuously filled with the precious Holy Spirit, but there are a thousand and one things that conspire to rob us of the sweetness and power of that state of living....

... The question is now, "Are we filled with the Holy Ghost?" ...

When we have grown cold, and a cloud has come between the soul and heaven, and our prayers do not get through any more, and we find ourselves drifting spiritually, there is only one remedy, and that is the blood of Jesus Christ. It isn't the Spirit we need—it is the blood. If we try to feel our way back to God we will miss it, because we cannot get back to God that way. The transforming power finds its source in the blood of Jesus Christ. Repentance and confession is the only road to the covering of the Blood. A change of life cannot come without repentance and the covering of the blood of Christ....

... If we are willing to judge ourselves, we will not be judged, but God will forgive, and through the merits of the precious blood we will be cleansed and purified and transformed. And the Holy Spirit will witness to the Blood and again we will be filled with the Holy Ghost....

If we are really filled with the Holy Spirit, praise will be spontaneous in our lives.... It bursts forth in psalms and hymns and spiritual songs, singing and making melody in the heart to the Lord. That is true evidence that one is filled with the Holy Spirit....

I feel sure that we all need to get closer to the cross of Calvary—we all need more of the cleansing power of the blood of the Lord Jesus Christ—we need to make a fuller, deeper consecration to Him, so that all our powers are dedicated unto His service. May we not be unwise, but understanding what the will of the Lord is. "And be not drunk with wine, wherein is excess; but be filled with the Spirit; speaking to yourselves in psalms and hymns and

"*One Great Christian Essential: 'Be Filled with the Spirit.'*"

spiritual songs, singing and making melody in your heart unto the Lord."

Excerpted from: J. Roswell Flower, "One Great Christian Essential: 'Be Filled with the Spirit,'" J. R. Flower at the Central Assembly of God, Springfield, Missouri, Sunday Morning, July 16, 1939," *Pentecostal Evangel* 1317 (August 5, 1939) 1, 4–5, 7. Used by permission of the General Council of the Assemblies of God.

Appendix D
"Spreading the Pentecostal Flames"

THE ONLY THING THAT will satisfy the heart of the believer is to be brought face-to-face with Christ in living fellowship. A shallow life will never produce this. That was the purpose of the tarrying meeting, which has almost gone out of existence in the Pentecostal movement. Tarrying in prayer is a necessity if we are to submit ourselves to the guidance and anointing of the Holy Spirit. God wants to come down upon His people in power and will do so if we will spend time in His presence and will seek His face with this fixed purpose.

Excerpted from: J. Roswell Flower, "Spreading the Pentecostal Flames," *Pentecostal Evangel* 2827 (July 14, 1968) 7–8. Used by permission of the General Council of the Assemblies of God.

Chronology

1888 born Joseph James Roswell Flower, Belleville, Ontario, Canada

1904 moved to Indianapolis, Indiana, with family

1907 accepted Jesus Christ and consecrated his life to Him at a Pentecostal mission

1909 received the baptism in the Holy Spirit, St. Louis, Missouri

1910 baptized in water at the Stone Church, Chicago, Illinois

1911 married Alice Marie Reynolds, Indianapolis, Indiana, June 1

1913 founded, published, and edited *Christian Evangel*

1914 attended inaugural meeting of the General Council of the Assemblies of God, Hot Springs, Arkansas, April 2–12; elected secretary

1919 elected first Secretary-Treasurer of newly approved Department of Missions

1925 moved to Scranton, Pennsylvania; pastor Pentecostal Assembly of God Church

1930 elected Superintendent of Eastern District; moved to Lititz, Pennsylvania

1935 elected General Secretary of the General Council; returned to Springfield, Missouri

Chronology

1943 participated in formation of the National Association of Evangelicals

1948 participated in World Pentecostal Conference and Pentecostal Fellowship of North America discussions; served in executive positions

1952 traveled to London for World Pentecostal Conference

1953 elected as councilman Springfield, Missouri, City Council

1954 traveled to London to help plan 1955 World Pentecostal Conference

1955 spoke at the World Pentecostal Conference in Stockholm, Sweden

1956 honored by Sertoma Club for "Service to Mankind"

1959 traveled to Europe, the Middle East, and India; retired from the General Secretary's office

1970 died, July 23

A Note on Sources

THERE ARE A FEW biographical sketches of J. Roswell Flower (some of these also include Alice Reynolds Flower) in reference works, pamphlets, magazine articles, histories of the Assemblies of God, surveys of Pentecostalism, and studies of American Religious history. No published full-length study exists. This biography is based largely on primary sources (published and unpublished) included in the Flower Family Papers (FFP). FFP is a collection of documents dating from the late-eighteenth century to the nineteen-eighties from both the Flower and Reynolds families. It contains letters, diaries, journals, manuscripts, sermon notes and outlines, datebooks, poems, genealogical information from family Bibles and professional services, newspaper clippings (usually unidentified), legal documents, and more, as well as copies of many published articles, booklets, tracts, poems, and devotional thoughts. FFP is held by Kathryn Flower Ringer (a granddaughter of J. Roswell Flower) and her husband, David K. Ringer. Additional sources in the Flower Pentecostal Heritage Center were used.

J. Roswell Flower (JRF)
c. 1900.

JRF c. 1904.

JRF and Alice Reynolds Flower (ARF) Wedding Day, June 1, 1911.

JRF and ARF mid-1950s.

JRF and Noel Perkin, Africa 1938.

JRF and ARF with children 1940. From left to right: George, Suzanne, JRF, Joseph, ARF, Rossie, Adele, David.

JRF at Central Bible Institute c. 1950.

Advisory Council for World Pentecostal Conference 1954. From left to right: Leonard Steiner (Switzerland), Samuel Nystrom (Sweden), JRF, Donald Gee (England), and Lewis Pethrus (Sweden).

JRF at John Bunyan's grave c. 1955. Pilgrim's Progress was one of JRF's favorite books.

JRF with five surviving children 1957. From left to right: Suzanne, Adele, David, George, JRF, Joseph.

JRF dedicating missionary Mark Buntain's church and school, India 1958.

JRF in academic regalia c. 1956.

JRF mid-1950s.

For Further Reading

Blumhofer, Edith L. *The Assemblies of God: A Chapter in the Story of American Pentecostalism.* 2 vols. Springfield, MO: GPH, 1989.
Burgess, Stanley M., et al., eds. *Dictionary of Pentecostal and Charismatic Movements.* Grand Rapids: Zondervan, 1988.
Flower, Alice Reynolds. *Grace for Grace: Some Highlights of God's Grace in the Daily Life of the Flower Family.* Springfield, MO: n.p., 1961.
McGee, Gary B. *People of the Spirit: The Assemblies of God.* Springfield, MO: GPH, 2004.
Menzies, Robert P. *Pentecost: This Story Is Our Story.* Springfield, MO: GPH, 2013.
Menzies, William W. *Anointed to Serve: The Story of the Assemblies of God.* Springfield, MO: GPH, 1971.
Menzies, William W., and Stanley M. Horton. *Bible Doctrines: A Pentecostal Perspective.* Springfield, MO: Logion, 1993.
Menzies, William W., and Robert P. Menzies. *Spirit and Power: Foundations of Pentecostal Experience.* Grand Rapids: Zondervan, 2000.
Ringer, David K. "J. Roswell Flower: Founding Father, Generous Spirit." DMin project, Assemblies of God Theological Seminary, 2014.

www.ingramcontent.com/pod-product-compliance
Lightning Source LLC
Chambersburg PA
CBHW050838160426
43192CB00011B/2070